Developing Consciousness

A Roadmap of the Journey
to Enlightenment

T0050606

For my mother
Thank you for everything

CONTENTS

Chapter 1: Consciousness and Reality

And then one day something miraculous happens...　　1

You are always in exactly the right place to be able

to take the next step..　　3

Become aware of what you are already aware of...　　5

Real wealth lies in our ability to appreciate

our experience...　　7

A concert pianist has to be able to play all

the notes on the piano, not just the ones

that come immediately to hand...　　14

Wisdom handed down by others tends

to be less useful than wisdom that

you have actually discovered yourself...　　17

We look at people and we think that

they think the same way that we think...　　19

You cannot help making decisions...　　22

We have all we need within ourselves. We

just have to become conscious of it....　　27

Chapter 2: The Mind

You are not your mind...　　34

A computer can never be spontaneous...　　37

We always have the power within

ourselves to change...　　39

The purpose of the mind is to survive...　　45

Persistent unwanted conditions...　　47

What is real for us is what our senses

tell us and what we observe...　　53

The power to determine the nature of

your reality still lies in your own hands...　　56

Move from looking at the *content* of our
    consciousness, to the *nature* of
    that consciousness...   61
The nature of Consciousness...   64
Consciously control yourself to observe the mind...   69

Chapter 3: Spirituality   72
A bridge to a new understanding...   78
We are not really interested in theories...   81
Divine Consciousness...   84
We all share a commonwealth,
    and that commonwealth is the Divine
    Consciousness that gives us everything...   87
You do not have to be enlightened to be enlightened...   90
Like a fish trying to describe a cash register...   92

Chapter 4: The Tradition of Mystical Reality
Just realise where you come from:
    This is the essence of wisdom...   95
Christianity should be considered
    as an 'Eastern religion'...   102
The more you know, the less you understand...   107

Chapter 5: Past, Present and Future   112
What has happened to us to shape
    us into the people we are today?...   114
Pain is our body's way of telling us
    that something is wrong...   116
A pair of fives is a winning hand...   121
Just take the next step, and then the one after that...   128
Books fall off shelves...   133
The reward for sitting in silence, is sitting in silence...   138
A portal into another dimension...   143
The important thing to do is to start...   149

Meditation...   152
All eternity seems to have become ours
      in this one placid and breathless contact...   157
Out of our sleep and into the wakefulness
      of full consciousness...   160

More Information   165
My Thanks   165
Booklist   166
Notes   168

There is the theory of life,
and then there is the actual practice of living it.
Theory without practice is mere speculation.
Practice without theory suggests irresponsibility.
When the two come together, one informs the other.

Chapter 1

Consciousness and Reality

And then one day something miraculous happens

Imagine your world as a house.

You can only move from room to room.

In all the time that anyone can ever remember no one has ever been Outside.

Outside. There are myths and legends of people that have seen what it looks like; tales of grass, and trees, of sky and sun.

Whole religions have been built up to explain how to get there, but you have never met anyone who has actually seen it.

Many people have come to the view that it does not exist. They get on with their lives within their own four walls. They are not interested in the speculation that many people fall prey to.

You, however, are interested in Outside.

You have heard the tales like everyone else, and are just as disenchanted with all the religions and the way they seem to explain everything without actually getting you anywhere.

And so you go on a search.

You ask, you read, you look around you.

And then one day something miraculous happens.

You are staring at one of the four walls in your room, when suddenly the wall seems to dissolve, and there it is in front of you – 'Outside', just like they said it would be. There are trees, clouds, the sun, fields, and acres and acres of space.

Wow!

You look in wonder and gaze upon this sacred sight that you have heard of so often, and, although you have never seen it before, you recognise all you see as what others have spoken of.

You know that this is what others have seen, you know it is real, and you know it is there.

Wow!

And then, suddenly the vision begins to fade. The wall comes back again and you are left, as before, in your room with its four walls.

You look about you. You see others in your room going about their business as if nothing had happened.

But you know.

You know there is such a thing as Outside. You know it exists, and yet you are living in a world where it is rarely acknowledged.

You are conscious of something that others are not.

The word "conscious" comes from two Latin words 'con' – together, and 'scios'- to know. To be con-scios is literally to know together.

Our mind takes all that it is fed, and makes a picture of what it knows.

Together as sentient beings we share with each other what we have come to know, and therefore as a race we begin to know together.

This book is offered on that basis. It is not 'what's so', it is just what I think I have seen as being so, and will only be useful to the extent that you test it against what you see as being so. Make your own mind up as to what you think *is* so, then decide what you are going to do with the information.

That is the trick when making a contribution in this area – acting on what you know.

Not with a view to being right, but with the willingness to be wrong.

Someone once asked the Dalai Lama what he would do if someone conclusively proved that reincarnation did not exist, and he said he would change his beliefs accordingly.

I offer this in that spirit – willing to be wrong.

Willing to change what I think is right, if you can tell me where I am going wrong.

You are always in exactly the right place to be able to take the next step

The journey Outside is the journey of enlightenment; and one of the reasons for writing this book is that the directions given for the journey to enlightenment are often so complicated.

Most traditions won't tell you where you are going.

They say that you will be told what you need to know, when you need to know it.

"There is no point in revealing the hidden truths of the tradition before you are ready to hear them," otherwise it is a case of "pearls before swine".

"The initiation will come when it is ready, and until then it is best to have the faith and the humility to be prepared not to know."

The problem is that most gatekeepers of this truth make it complicated because they themselves have never experienced it, and so all they can do is to make a virtue out of travelling the road, rather than arriving.

Life becomes a process of readying for something that never actually appears.

We become trapped in ever more complicated processes and lifestyles that are supposed to be leading us along the way, but in fact wear us down to the point where we do not care whether we arrive or not. We are simply grateful to be on the journey.

And, of course, this method does eventually work, because the moment we give up really wanting to arrive, then we stop seeking, we empty ourselves of all the ideas we have about what that arrival might be, and, lo and behold, we find ourselves home. Outside. In that place we have been seeking.

But that is another story.

Each of us has the secret of how to get Outside, how to become enlightened, within us.

It is just a question of allowing it to come out. And the approach that this book takes is to describe that process as simply as possible, so that you can at least know the territory of Outside, and therefore be able to recognise it when you come across it.

The problem comes when we try too hard to engage with where we are, and where we are trying to get to.

Two travellers came upon a farmer at his gate as they walked down the road.

"Can you tell me the way to the great city?" one of the travellers asked.

"Sure," the farmer answered, "but if I was going to the great city, I would not want to be starting from here."

Many of us feel that about the way we are in our lives.

We think that we have to get somewhere else to be able to start.

To be in the right place, wherever that might be.

So here is **"Realisation number one"** about learning to get Outside in your life:

You are always in exactly the right place to be able to take the next step.

And it is an amazing realisation, that you are, right now, in exactly the right place to begin this journey.

Your whole life has brought you to this point. Everything you have ever done has brought you to the point of reading these words now. And everything has conspired for you to be in exactly the right place. You could not be in a better place.

And that is true for every single moment of your life.

You are never in the wrong place. All you can do is to not recognise you are in the right place, and then automatically you miss the point and opportunity of that moment.

To be in the right place at the right time you simply have to acknowledge the rightness of the moment, and thus the moment becomes yours.

Do it now. Without qualification.

Whatever your circumstances, wherever you are. Trust this moment as being one that is right. One that has meaning. One that is setting you on a journey Outside the box, and it will be so.

And what is the next step? Well, ask yourself that – what is the next step? What do you do right now as the next step?

Become aware of what you are already aware of

Well, for some of you the next step was to continue reading. For others it was to do something else. But given that you are reading this now, it has to mean that you are still on that journey, and that right now is again the perfect place to be for the next step.

That is the great thing about the journey Outside. There really are no wrong steps, so long as you acknowledge that you are on the journey, and your intention is to continue.

So here we are.

Hopefully, this book does what it says on the can.

It is simply about 'Developing Consciousness'. About both becoming more conscious of what is around us, what is in us, and what we are up to – as well as becoming aware of the nature of our consciousness. Most of which we tend to take for granted.

Because we do take our consciousness for granted.

We say, "I am conscious, now what can I discover about life?"

"What can I learn about what is out there to make me feel better about what is in here?"

Which is really the wrong way round.

Surely a better way would be to say, "I am conscious. What is it that I can learn about the nature of my consciousness that will tell me more about what I perceive to be out there?"

100% of our life is made up of our consciousness, and yet we hardly ever examine it.

What does it mean to see? To really see, not just to look and observe, but to take in the marvellousness of sight. The miracle of seeing. The wonder of colours, of light and shade, of shapes and contours.

But no, our reality is more on the lines of, "There is the bus, here is my money, there is the seat, who are all those awful people round me?"

We might *really see* if we are in exceptional circumstances, but most of the time we are just looking as to what is going to come next.

And that goes for all our other senses that make up our consciousness.

So the next step in developing your consciousness is to become aware of what you are already aware of.

To become aware of all the things that make up your consciousness.

Our hearing, like the other senses, has been relegated to mere usefulness with the odd moment of genuine appreciation.

We often don't *really* hear. Ask a blind person how much sighted people miss. The nuances of voices in a conversation, the shift in atmosphere in a room as someone enters, the change in pressure before rain comes.

We have lost it in our desire to get on to the main business of living life. Our consciousness has become a means to an end, when really it is the end in itself.

What else is there? – everything comes to us through our consciousness. Name me one thing that does not.

There is a huge variety of touch and sensation – capable of everything from the most orgasmic eruption of sensuality, to the gentlest of breezes on open skin.

All the time it is registering information, and yet most of it is never consciously appreciated. Every time we stand, sit, touch something, feel heat or cold, feel wet, feel the sun on our faces or the wind on our backs. All the time that information is coming to us, most of it goes unregistered.

Notice what you are feeling right now.

The sensation in your bottom if you are sitting? What can you feel? What is the temperature like, what do your clothes feel like? Notice it now and register it.

And notice that you are thinking about it - another part of your consciousness. Thoughts, memories, dreams and reflections are all a part of what it is to be conscious. But how often do we really become conscious of what we are thinking? Most of the time we merely make deductions and move on. We do not say, "That was interesting I thought that... I notice I am thinking this..." ...being conscious of the thought, rather than making deductions about it.

So gradually we can build up a picture of that which we call our consciousness – senses, thought, even a sense of 'self'. They are all part of what we are conscious of, but we never question them. We simply use them as we go about our lives.

In considering this we begin to get a sense of the huge resource we have at our disposal in the nature of our consciousness, but which we have taken for granted.

Here lies all answers to who we are and what our purpose in life is.

Real wealth lies in our ability to appreciate our experience

All the steps we are taking are ways of developing our consciousness.

If we are not interested in developing our consciousness we just carry on life as normal, moving from one thing to the next, making the best of life that we can. Working out which job, which activity, which person is going to make our lives richer.

The purpose of getting money is presumably to enable us to live more fulfilled and more secure lives.

It is always interesting then to see very wealthy people who live pretty miserable lives.

There is an old adage that says if you are going to be miserable, it is better to be miserable rich than miserable poor.

And it is a cliché to say that money cannot buy you happiness (or love). But why is that?

The key is to realise that our real wealth lies in our ability to appreciate our experience.

If we are not able to appreciate the wonderful glories of the sights and sounds that are around us, to fully feel the joy of being alive, even fully feel the richness of grief, then no amount of money will make any difference to us. We will simply use our money to distract us from the poverty we feel in our lives. It takes so much to make a difference to the way we feel that we have to spend more and more on vastly elaborate ways of distracting us from the poverty of our experience.

Look at one moment through the eyes of an experience of poverty:

I got out of the car, walked down the street, went into a bar and ordered a cup of coffee.

When we are experiencing life to the minimum; when we have a consciousness that is poverty stricken, that is how such a brief moment may unfold.

Add the richness of a consciousness that is aware of itself and its surroundings and it might go something like this:

As I got out of the car I was immediately hit by the heat, and a smell of wood smoke that threw me back to my childhood in Nepal.
All around me the pavement thronged with schools of whirling robes and burkas as men and women animatedly argued about anything

and everything. Children shrieked and laughed through games using tin cans and old tyres.

I immediately felt exposed as a stranger.

Seemingly careless eyes appraised me and found me wanting. I should not be there, so near the mosque at such a sacred time.

Fear began to seep through my skin and make its way towards my heart. I had to get off the street, out of sight, anywhere but here.

I dived into the nearest bar. The cool of the air conditioning struck me like an open fridge and darkness evaporated before me as my eyes became accustomed to the dimness of the light.

I stumbled towards the bar and pointed desperately at the coffee machine. I needed something to hide behind, and a cup of coffee was the only camouflage available.

Two descriptions of the same thing.

One empty of experience, one filled with the sights, sounds and senses of life. One poor, one rich.

We have the same choices in our life. To live life as a drab continuum. Going from bed to work (or not), a couple of meals, back home, telly and then bed again. Or feeling all the vibrancy of life as we live through it.

You cannot buy that vibrancy. The more money you throw at it, the less you are able to really feel it.

Developing consciousness brings that richness to our lives. The first step is an acknowledgement of the amazingness of life as we live it. The sheer miracle of actually being alive. Of being able to make sense of the world that is around us.

We take being alive for granted.

We have got used to it. Over the years it has become no big deal. We have been around for so long that we no longer appreciate where we are and what is available to us.

Admit it to yourself. See it in those who are around you. It is a natural state. Life goes on, and we have to suffer the ordinariness of washing up, as well as the relatively rare joys that come our way, along with the slings and arrows of outrageous fortune.

I found this story on the Internet:

A group of students were asked to list what they thought were the current Seven Wonders of the World. Though there was some disagreement, the following got the most votes:

1. Egypt's Great Pyramids
2. Taj Mahal
3. Grand Canyon
4. Panama Canal
5. Empire State Building
6. St. Peter's Basilica
7. China's Great Wall

While gathering the votes, the teacher noted that one quiet student hadn't turned in her paper yet. So she asked the student if she was having trouble with her list. The girl replied, "Yes, a little. I couldn't quite make up my mind because there were so many." The teacher said, "Well, tell us what you have, and maybe we can help." The girl hesitated, then read, "I think the Seven Wonders of the World are:

1. to touch
2. to taste
3. to see
4. to hear
5. to feel
6. to laugh
7. and to love."

The room was full of silence.

Aged 11 – "You always wanted to get mail"

The Royal Mail is something that was of crucial importance at a boarding school. It was the lifeline from home: bringing presents, comics and other things that eased the burden of confinement.

The post was given out in the morning at assembly. One of the senior boys sat on a large radiator at the side of the gym with a pile of letters.

"Franks," he shouted.

"Here," came the response, and the letter was propelled across the room to the vicinity where Franks sat. After a bit of a scuffle the letter eventually ended up in Franks' hands.

"Pangbourne." "Here," and a rolled comic (it is ingenious how they used to roll and mail comics) somersaulted though the air with considerable force right into Pangbourne's hands. The prefects always prided themselves on the accuracy of their throwing.

You always wanted to get mail. There was no downside: Bills did not exist for us, and if there was any really bad news it was conveyed, sensitively, through the headmaster.

You always wanted to get mail.

If you read the national newspapers carefully you will notice that a considerable number of advertisements carry ways of responding. In the days before the Internet most of that responding was done by post.

At the bottom of each ad there was a coupon to clip. "Send for our annual report now"… "and fill in your name and address for a catalogue."

Anyway, someone at the school was reading their papers carefully, and they noticed.

And soon others noticed that this particular boy was getting quite a bit of post in the mornings. They saw that they too could get post just by filling in a coupon and sending off an envelope to a freepost address.

The craze was on and the school's daily delivery went from an armful of letters to an entire mailbag in a matter of weeks.

It took three times as long to hand out the post every morning.

And if you looked in boys' lockers you would see a stack of annual reports from some of the most well-known companies in the country.

Another institution at boarding school is prep.

Every weekday evening all the boys are assembled in classrooms for an hour, in silence, to do their homework. As we had no homes to go to, this was called preparation, or prep.

Generally one master looked after prep.

The classrooms were of all ranges around a central hall, and with all the doors left open the one master could control the 100 boys in his charge. The rest of them being either day boys or too young for prep and already in bed.

We could always track the master by his footsteps. Like a radar, we could plot his course in our heads so that by the time he got round to our classroom we were all in pre-prepared positions of studious work.

At the back of the hall was a corridor. If you heard footsteps coming down that corridor you knew that something was up because that led the way to the headmaster's apartments, or 'Privateside' as it was called. You only went there by invitation; and then always with a sense of dread. Very little good news came out of Privateside.

This particular night there was a sudden alert. Joining the regular plod of the duty master's footsteps was the unmistakable noise of the headmaster coming down the corridor and into the hall through the door at the back of the room.

No one moved, but all of us watched with the eyes in the back of our heads (to turn round was to invite trouble) as the headmaster *gradually came into view.*

He walked straight up to the duty master who had also heard the steps and the two of them conferred in hushed voices at the front of the room.

I knew something was up when they both looked up and stared straight at me. I froze, paralysed to the bench.

'The headmaster called my name, and then just walked off.

By the time I had scrabbled to my feet and got up, the headmaster was out of the hall.

As I turned into the corridor I saw him a few yards ahead of me striding towards Privateside.

I followed him in that half-walk, half-run that children use when they are trying to keep up with an adult's stride. I felt sick.

By the time I got to the big door that delineated our area from Privateside and pushed my way through, the hall in front of me was deserted. There was a big circular table surrounded by three doors, all closed. I made my way to the one that I knew to be the headmasters study.

I knocked feebly,

"Come in."

I opened the door and walked in.

I knew there was trouble, because the headmaster was not alone. He sat at his desk, but at the other side of the room stood a man in a raincoat and a flat cap. He did not look happy. It was raining outside and he was wet.

My fears grew as the headmaster did not even bother to address me, but turned to the man instead.

"Mr. Longstreet, this is the young man that you have driven down from London to sell a washing machine to."

Having said this, the headmaster turned to me.

"You may now go."

I never saw that man again.

I turned and left the room and wandered in a state of overwhelming dread back to the school. I could not conceive of a punishment that would adequately fit the crime I had seemingly committed, although I had absolutely no knowledge of how that man had come to darken my door. Unless someone had filled in a coupon with my name on it....

My response was to go straight to the communal baths and throw up in one of the basins.

The next morning, at breakfast, the headmaster addressed the school.

The practice of filling in coupons in newspapers was to stop. Last night there had been an unfortunate incident which did not show the school in a good light.

No more would be said about it, and that would be the end of it.

And so it was.

Despite the heinous nature of my supposed crime, there was no punishment, and the school delivery of mail went back to its customary armful.

A concert pianist has to be able to play all the notes on the piano, not just the ones that come immediately to hand

It is amazing to think of all the aspects that make up our consciousness.

Imagine you have created a human being, but without any aspects of consciousness, just the flesh and bones. What would you give your human to bring them into full consciousness?

If you have a moment, take a pen and paper and list all the functions of consciousness that you can think of giving your creature.

Now compare with the list below.

Functions of Consciousness

Sight

There is a huge variation in sight, from depth, to colour to dimension.

Sound

Including everything from music to the telephone ring, vibration, a sense of balance. Whales find their way around through sound.

Smell

Said to be the oldest of the senses in that the sperm is supposed to find its way to the egg through smell. Also the sense of smell is linked to memory. Walk into a classroom and find yourself transported back to your own school life. Again animals use this sense much more than we do. It is linked to taste.

Taste

Sweet, sour, bitter, salty. The huge variety of tastes available to show us what to eat and what to avoid.

Touch

Hot and cold, pain and pleasure. Being able to feel our way around life. Sensations telling us what will be good for us and what will harm us.

Other body sensations

Everything from hunger to the need to pee, itches, sexuality, funny bone, and balance.

Conscious thought

Memory, reason, instinct.

Mental Imagery

Imagination, colour, patterns.

Emotions

Love, joy, peace, apathy, grief, fear, anger, pride.

Sense of Self

Some kind of overall experience of who we are.

This is not an exhaustive list, but just some ideas to see the range of aspects that go to make up your consciousness. Then there are all the combinations of these aspects. Like regret, guilt, anticipation, exhilaration. It is an endless list, and it is the wealth that you have at your fingertips.

It is through being aware of these experiences that you begin to see the extent of your consciousness and the amount you take it for granted. Most of the time you do not think about it, you just carry on feeling less and less, and thinking that there must be more, somewhere.

It may be obvious, but the first step on the road to Outside has to be cultivating an appreciation of everything that you have on the inside.

You cannot expect this enlightenment to compensate for some lack that you are currently experiencing. It has to lead out of the richness and abundance that you are already in possession of.

Simple as it may be, you have to become aware of everything that is currently available to you, before you can go further.

A concert pianist has to be able to play **all** the notes on the piano, not just the ones that come immediately to hand.

He has to move his hands up and down the keys, stretching his fingers to find more and more complicated combinations of notes to make up the intricate melodies and chords.

Only then, when he has mastered the instrument, can he expect to do justice to Rachmaninov's 3rd piano concerto. Only then will the majesty of the instrument become apparent to him.

And so it is with us.

Only when we have mastered our ability to experience what is already available to us will we be able to grasp what is available outside that capacity.

Most of us are nowhere near being open to experiencing at full capacity, and have no desire to reach it.

And I am not talking about white-water rafting, or bungee jumping. I am referring to the extra-ordinary that is available to us within the ordinariness of our every day lives. Until we can make that extra-ordinary, we cannot expect to receive more.

Wisdom handed down by others tends to be less useful than wisdom that you have actually discovered yourself

The International Dictionary of Psychology[1] defines consciousness as, *"The having of perceptions, thoughts, and feelings; awareness. The term is impossible to define except in terms that are unintelligible without a grasp of what consciousness means. Consciousness is a fascinating but elusive phenomenon: it is impossible to specify what it is, what it does, or why it evolved. Nothing worth reading has been written about it. (Sutherland 1989)"*

Well, apart from the fact that it calls into question whether a book like this is worth reading or not – How amazing!

A scientific definition that actually puts us in the driving seat, which allows us to be experts over our own understanding of our lives. Because of course *we are* the people to work out what our consciousness means, and what it tells us about the nature of living. Because that is surely the point of this exercise.

A Buddhist once said to me that the purpose of his practice was to live life more skilfully – what a perfect definition of why we go about developing our consciousness. Surely the reason is that we might live life more skilfully. That we might find the right places to put our feet as we climb the mountains that are our lives. That we might build our lives on solid foundations.

Just as an architect designs a building taking into consideration the laws of gravity, so we have to take into consideration the laws that make up the living of life.

Once we have discovered what we can rely on, we can put our feet firmly on those places and move on to the next place.

Developing consciousness is working out what we can really rely upon. What is not going to give way when we put our weight on it. What we can trust.

We have to get an understanding of the nature of reality.

The science fiction author Philip K. Dick defined reality as, "that which, when you stop believing in it, doesn't go away."[2]

And I think that is useful.

We are trying to work out what is really there, and what is an illusion, whether or not we have a firmly held belief that it does exist.

Which is why it is good to use the concept of "Con-Sciosness".

Why it is good to work out what all our senses, body sensations and our thoughts are telling us, and measure that in a conscios way against what other people are saying that their senses and body sensations are telling them. Then we begin to get an idea of what is real.

And that it is not just what you have read and agree with.

So much of what we think about in relationship to our living comes from us second hand. Ideas that others have had that seem to be right to us. We then take on those ideas without really examining them. We say, "OK I will take this on," and then you try to add something else to the picture and it doesn't quite fit – so you come back to the original conceptualisation and you say to it, "This bit does not fit," and that worldview says, "well, maybe not, but if you look at it this way it does seem to fit better," and before you know it you are not thinking for yourself, you are just taking on someone else's pre-thought-through worldview.

And every time there is a bit that does not fit your worldview, you have to admit that it is your thinking that is wrong, and adapt to the worldview that you have unconsciously taken on.

And soon we are trapped and ALL our thinking becomes referenced to a particular worldview. We have bought into it completely, and all we can do is adjust our thinking when we find ourselves in conflict.

We become powerless to work things out for ourselves.

It is important to begin with your consciousness, begin with what

you know. Then look at what others tell you that *they* know from their consciousness (as opposed to what they believe) and then you can begin to build up a picture that is your own: one that is authentic, that puts you in the driving seat.

Which is not to say that it is wrong to read, or wrong to take ideas from others. Just that you have to question how much of your creative faculties you are giving up to others. How much of the power to actualise and create your life you have invested in a thought franchise created by someone else.

A franchise that you have bought into and that has rules and regulations that you have to obey if the franchise is going to work for you.

Many of these franchises do work. They enable people to make sense of their lives, to feel secure and to build in conjunction with others.

But before you buy into them it is important to understand your own make-up. What is true for you, and therefore what you can rely on.

Wisdom handed down by others tends to be less useful than wisdom that you have actually discovered yourself.

We look at people and we think that they think the same way that we think

So how do we make up our reality?

Well, obviously we take information given to us by our senses and we work out what is going on from this information.

When you pick something up with your sight, smell, sound or any one of your senses it impacts on the sensory receptors in the brain. You then organise the information to build up a picture of what is happening.

You are in a shop. There is fish on the counter in front of you, there is a man standing there with an apron on, you can smell the fish, you can see the prices on the fish, you can remember going to this shop before, you can see a shopping list in front of you with the word "FISH" on it, and you know that you are in a shop about to buy fish and act accordingly.

The problem comes when you receive various pieces of information and come to the wrong conclusion. To take the example above, the key piece of information you have forgotten is that you are an actor in a film, this is a set, and you are not there to buy fish, but to kill the fishmonger for something that they did to you years ago.

But you have to remember that you are not going to actually kill the fishmonger, you are only going to pretend to kill him, because this is a film and you are an actor, and the other actor has a family he wants to get back to.

So you are not there to shop and there is other information which, if not heeded, will lead you in the wrong direction.

Much of our pain is due to the fact that we misread the signals that life is telling us about what is really going on.

Developing consciousness is about becoming conscious of as much as is possible of that which is in your reality, so that you can get a clear picture of what is going on and act accordingly.

Because we assume so much.

We think others think in the same way that we do.

We look at people and we think that they think the same way that we think.

I'll give you an example. It is a small exercise that you can do exactly where you are right now.

I am going to ask you to think about something: March 5th this year. Think about that date.

Now I am going to ask you to think about another date. January 26th last year.

Now think of July 16th next year

Now December this year.

How do you think about time?

Well I'll tell you how I think about it.

I think of time in a circular fashion going anticlockwise. December ends on the hour, and January till June goes back to a quarter-to, July till September goes back to about twenty-five past the hour, October to December up to the hour.

Anticlockwise, with different parts of the year taking more time on the clock face than others.

So, March 5th is somewhere between ten-to and five-to the hour.

For January 26th last year we have to go clockwise once round to get there, then for July 16th next year you have to go anticlockwise all the way through last year, past the hour into this year the same way, and up to July 16th next year.

For December this year we go from where we are now, anticlockwise up to the hour.

Simple eh! But it is how I think about it.

I think about time as a spiral that goes anticlockwise as it progresses.

How did you think about it?

When I have tried this on groups I get a whole host of answers. A horizontal linear construction left to right, or sometimes right to left, or vertical up and down, or from the back through the body and out through the front, or spiral clockwise, or pictorially in seasons, or as a calendar on the wall, or as colours. Any number of constructions.

All of us conceptualise time in very different ways.

And that is just time. Something we all experience in a pretty similar way. Something that we all agree on as to its end points and the way that it operates in our lives.

Just imagine the variety of ways of thinking about the concept of 'peace'. The different nuances it has for each one of us. Or even "love". Is it any wonder that so many lovers end up splitting up when you think of the different ways we all understand those three words "I love you"? Each of us will have a completely different understanding of what that means. We apply the word to our own lives, our own experience of love, or lack of it.

What can we expect from people that say "I love you"? How do we respond to them? What are they expecting of us? It is all such a complete mess it is amazing that so many couples manage to stay together and work it all out.

All of us experience consciousness, and have an understanding of the nature of reality based upon that consciousness. But how do we deal with the fact that our understanding of reality does not always tally with the way that others understand it?

You cannot help making decisions

Well the answer is that we have to go deeper into our consciousness and look harder at the software that is working out what is going on – namely The Mind.

We have to begin to look at our minds. To begin to observe our minds while they are working, and look at what decisions they are making.

Because your mind is always making decisions. It has made a decision about what it thinks about this book. About me, the writer. It is making decisions all the time about everything. And most of the time you are completely unconscious about the decisions you are making.

You just make them and move on.

"That bloke on the train with a beard – what a creep. I bet he likes heavy metal and has got piercings all over his body."

And of course you have no idea who he is or what he does. But you make decisions anyway.

"That woman at work – how sad. No partner or children. I bet she just sits at home watching TV all day."

You have no idea.

But, hang on – surely you who are reading this book are more enlightened about life than this. You don't judge in this way do you?

But consider the judgement that you made about the fact that you are not the sort of person that makes judgements. Isn't that a judgement in itself?

We do it all the time.

It is how we live our lives. We decide which way to walk to work. Which coffee to buy, who to buy it from, when to drink it, what we think of it, what to do with the cup. What we think about people who do not put the cups in the bin. What we think about overcrowded bins. About bin collectors and their lives, and about people who live in those sorts of houses, about... about... about... about this paragraph, about whether you are going to read the next line, or the next chapter or ......

You cannot help making decisions. All you can do is become more conscious about the decisions you are making, and then decide if you really do want to make those decisions after all.

Because many of the decisions we make are wrong. They are wrong decisions based upon wrong assumptions based upon incorrect or incomplete information, that lead us to travel down the wrong paths in life.

We all do it, we cannot help it. But we can become conscious of it. Developing consciousness about the way you make decisions, and what you do about them, is a key aspect of learning to live more skilfully.

Because unless you see what decisions you are making, you cannot choose whether or not you want to act on those decisions.

Being aware of your decision-making does not mean you abandoning your critical faculties, but seeing those faculties in action, and then making the choice about whether or not to act upon them.

Because so many of the decisions we make are unconscious decisions. We are unaware of the fact that we are making them.

We automatically steel ourselves for dealing with the street beggar.

We have a raft of decisions that we have already made and which enable us to have a default position that we adopt when we are confronted by one.

This person is either genuine, or he is going to rip us off.

By giving ourselves these two choices and making a decision, we enable ourselves to act.

Think about the word "decide". If homicide is killing a person, fratricide is killing your brother, "de-ciding" is killing off the alternatives. There may be alternatives other than the two we have given ourselves: What does it mean to "rip someone off"? What is a genuine need? Is it not genuine when the person wants money for drugs or alcohol? What makes it more genuine if the person wants the money for food or accommodation? Surely both cases show need. You have to be pretty desperate to be begging on the street in the first place.

Does drug dependency disqualify people from our care?

I remember coming towards a street person once and trying to decide whether or not to give him money. He looked pretty worse for wear. Would he just spend the money on alcohol?

As I was struggling with the question the man stood up and walked towards me and thrust five pounds into my hand.

My mind was thrown into confusion as I tried to weigh up the situation:

Did I look so scruffy that he thought I needed the money? Had he found the money and was trying to find the owner? Had I so misread the situation?

"Excuse me sir," he said, "but would you mind going into the shop over there and buying me four cans of Special Brew? The shopkeeper won't serve me."

I was so shocked that I meekly took the money and carried out his wish.

Aged 12 – "You shot it, you kill it"

We sailed down the road on our bikes arguing over who should go in front. Park Road in Camberley was fairly busy as it took the traffic out of town and on to what was later to be the M3.

My brother, aged 10, was in front. I went to overtake and swerved out, picking up speed.

I was vaguely aware of the moped crashing as it veered into the centre of the road to miss me, skidding some 10 yards in front of me on its side as my brother fell off his bike.

I carried on peddling. I turned left on to a side road and started up the hill. I wanted to get away as fast as I could. If I put it out of my mind, then it was as if it had not happened. I rationalised my way out of the situation... then I stopped, turned round and let the bike coast me back to my fate.

In the end we walked our bikes home, not daring to be on the road again. My mother said she heard us saying as we came up the drive: "You tell her," "No you tell her."

Mrs Laramie, for it was she on the moped, ended up in hospital with a broken wrist, and my mother ended up paying the bill. No further action was taken.

We were not unhappy. But there again you could not exactly say we were happy. As boys we amused ourselves in the way boys do, with guns and explosives.

We managed to buy a smoke bomb in Hamleys. We got it in my bedroom, closed the door and lit it.

It fizzed and puffed and eventually began to bring forth smoke, and yet more smoke.

My brother and I began coughing and soon had to leave the

room. The smoke followed us. It seemed never to stop.

Eventually the three of us, my mother, my brother and myself, ended up on the front lawn looking up at the house as smoke poured out of all the upstairs windows.

I amused myself by putting my fingers in the socket of my bedside lamp. It made my arm throb.

As it was an interesting and not unappealing feeling I thought I owed it to my brother to stick his fingers in the light socket too. He was less pleased with the effect.

We bought a starting pistol, the sort used for athletics. You could buy them in sports shops. They were small thin silver guns that took an encased silver pellet that looked a bit like a nipple. We found that if you put them on the concrete ground and tapped them lightly with a hammer, you could build up the compression so that they made a hell of a bang.

However, our pride and joy were our air rifles. I owned a "Paratrooper", which, as well as having a stock, also had a pistol grip.

We fired at anything – targets, trees, the house and each other.

I found out that it could kill when I took aim at a pigeon that was sitting on a branch just above our garage.

I went for the body and pulled the trigger. It jumped in the air, and then fell to the ground.

I eventually found it. It was trapped in a small gap between our garage and the next door neighbour's fence. The gap was about a foot across, and it was inaccessible from either end. The pigeon flapped about.

I took aim and fired another shot. A burst of feathers and the pigeon rolled on to its side with its face pressed against the chicken wire that enclosed the gap between the garage and the fence.

Its beak was open and full of blood. I looked in horror, helpless. I went into the house, and got my mother and showed her.

I said, "I don't know what to do." She said, "You shot it, you kill it."

I tried another shot but still it would not die. My panic mounted as it seemed to wink at me with a horrifying intimacy.

Finally I managed to put the barrel of the gun against its head, and that finished it off.

I cannot work out why I did not learn from life's little lessons. I continued to shoot anything that came my way, but was always too squeamish and cowardly to ever finish them off by hand.

Later in life I used a shotgun, and while in Australia I used a 247 rifle to kill both birds and pigs.

It was something about seeing the effect I could have by inflicting power over helpless creatures, but not being willing to take responsibility for the pain and mess that was left in my wake.

We have all we need within ourselves. We just have to become conscious of it.

So, we have come quite a way in a short space of time.

We are saying that the purpose of developing consciousness is to enable us to live more skilfully.

That we have to begin the process by becoming conscious of those things that we take for granted – our senses, our thoughts, our decisions as we make them.

Actually, that is everything. That is the whole of the process of developing consciousness.

If we followed this to its logical conclusions we would arrive at the meaning of all life.

Because it is there. It is in our senses, in our thoughts and in the decisions we make. All of our living experience exists there.

Even the loftiest of lofty experiences and the deepest of deep truths have to come to us by way of our consciousness. It cannot come to us by any other way. Because our consciousness is all we have to work out what is going on in life.

In simple mode it tells us that water is wet and that rocks are hard. It enables us to know what blue looks like and what joy feels like.

It enables us to feel love, and respond to that love.

It enables us to laugh and cry.

But it also brings to us the secrets of eternal life.

There is no add-on that we have to download and apply. There is no place that we have to go to. No intermediary we have to hook up with. No equipment we have to get.

You have everything you need within you. Your consciousness contains all that you need in order to penetrate the most obscure truth about the nature of reality.

And yet we doubt ourselves.

We say that we need to find this master. To go on this pilgrimage. To read that book. To buy this crystal. To use these spells. To take this drug. To belong to this religion. To be a part of that group. To go through this portal which will take us into that dimension.

No.

We have everything you need within us. Our consciousness contains all that we need in order to penetrate the most obscure truth about the nature of reality.It is all about recollection, rather than finding something outside of ourselves.

Re-collection. Going into ourselves and re-collecting that which we already have. Information that we always had, but have largely forgotten.

It is a bit like our DNA. All of us have DNA unique to ourselves. It has enabled us to grow the way we have grown: our legs, our arms, our eyes. All of it comes down to our particular sequencing.

And it is the same with our consciousness. All of it will come down to a particular nature of reality that we can experience, but which we do not experience on a daily basis.

We are aware of what is around us as we look and see and hear. But there is more.

Cats see more than us, dogs hear more, so there must be more.

Developing consciousness is about exploring what that more might be.

And we have all the tools we need at our fingertips to undergo that exploration.

The capacity that enables you to see a table, hear a song, and feel love, is the same capacity that can enable you to see into the deepest mystery, to hear unimaginable sounds, and to feel out the true nature of reality.

The trick is to decide to use those faculties for that purpose.

Most of us are content to go from A to B. From birth and through life trying to become successful, raise a family, be comfortable, and do all the things that normal people do.

And we are all just normal people. Regular people who are just trying to get on in life.

And just like regular people we feel that maybe this is not all there is. That there might be more than the normal treadmill of life.

This must be something that you feel, otherwise you wouldn't be reading this book.

That is the first step. To acknowledge the feeling that there might be more. The next step is to explore what that more might be.

To actually make the effort to begin to look inward at what makes up your consciousness, your reality. How it comes about. How it works, and what part you play in its development.

To do that, you have to begin to look at the beliefs that you have grown up with. To look at how they were formed, and what has gone to make you the person you are. It will be a different story for each one of us; and yet there are common elements that we can share and "con-scios", know together.

And to do this we have to suspend our judgements. To be aware of the decisions we have made about life – what alternatives we have killed off – and be prepared to re-examine those alternatives to see if there is anything we can learn from them.

Aged 19 – "We'd get rid of it later"

I awoke to the sight of a mounted policeman towering above me. He was armed with a small pistol and dressed in the light blue regalia and peaked cap of the Dutch police.

I nervously reached for the Mars bar-sized chunk of dope in my pocket. Then I relaxed and remembered that I had slept overnight in Amsterdam's Vondelpark, where smoking cannabis was tolerated to the extent that coffee houses actually offered different varieties of the drug on menus.

There were eight of us in two cars. A Mini Moke (a mini with the roof and doors removed) and an old beat-up VW. It was two weeks of freedom after school, driving around France, Germany, Belgium and Holland.

We had brought tents and basic cooking gear.

To begin with we observed the rules and customs of whichever country we were in, however, as the days went past we gradually degenerated: Driving around Germany talking loudly about the war, getting drunk and generally descending into the worst that our characters were capable of expressing.

It came to a head one morning. Having camped in a forest, we drove out and came across a car that had obviously skidded off the road, gone over the verge and down the side of a small embankment. It had come to rest on its side, leaning against a tree some ten meters into a wood.

We got out to inspect. No one was in the car, and it was intact.

It was a small four door, maybe a Renault or a Peugeot. We circled it, looking inside. It was empty.

You could almost feel the wildness build within the group. Then suddenly one of us picked up a log and drove it through the windscreen, shattering it.

Someone else broke the back windows and soon every window in the car was smashed.

Next the wing mirrors were ripped off their mountings and the doors were opened and pushed back on their hinges until they broke.

In a frenzy of destruction we completely trashed the vehicle in about 10 minutes.

We then got back into our cars and drove off.

Afterwards no one mentioned what had happened, but it was obvious to us all that a low point had been reached, and that the only solution was to head for Amsterdam and "get out of it".

It was our last couple of days. We scored more easily than we could have imagined.

Eight boys not quite believing that you really could smoke dope out in the open and no one would challenge you.

We bought far too much and we smoked it until we could barely move. We agreed that we would throw it away when we left Amsterdam.

But on the day of our departure we just couldn't do it.

We'd get rid of it later.

Half way to the ferry we stopped at a roadside lay-by and lit up. Some time later the picnic bench was littered with bodies. Some slumped across the table; others lying on the ground – all of us completely wasted.

Eventually we got it together to drive off towards the Hook of Holland, where we would embark for Harwich. We'd get rid of the stuff there.

It is hard to throw away something that is normally so difficult to get hold of, at least in England.

So there we were again, on the ferry, blasted.

Things were coming to a head, and we knew that we would have to throw it overboard before we got to the UK.

But we didn't, after all what we still had left was worth at least £100.

We decided that the Mini Moke was too obvious, and that we were bound to get stopped, so the dope was to go in the VW.

As the ferry docked we got into our cars and were soon rolling down the ramp.

I was in the Mini Moke and we got off first, followed by the VW immediately behind. We twisted down and drove into the queue for passports.

No problem there, and so on towards the customs bay.

The guard waved us through.

As we passed we saw the VW being moved into one of the inspection bays.

Disaster.

We drove out of the port area, turned right and parked up about 200 yards from the entrance.

The engine stopped and there was complete silence.

"We'll pay the fine for them," someone said.

"And visit them every week in prison."

None of us could quite get a hold on the enormity of what had happened.

Arrest would lead to a court case, conviction and jail. It would ruin their lives.

We all felt a mixture of guilt at what we had done, and relief that we were not the ones in trouble.

We sat in silence and waited, trying to work out what had actually happened and what we were going to do about it.

After what seemed like an age one of us saw it.

The battered yellow VW edging its way out of the port gates and slowly making its way towards us.

"What happened?"

"Oh nothing really, they just waved us from one bay to the next, and then eventually we found ourselves on the way out. Pretty lucky wasn't it."

Chapter 2

The Mind

You are not your mind

Monopolies are not a particularly good idea, unless you own the monopoly. Which is why, by and large, governments legislate against them.

Monopolies tend to promote the interests of the company over the individual. There is very little balance that can come from the marketplace.

In the marketplace of your life your mind has a monopoly over you.

You only have one mind, and it generally tells you what to do.

We think of ourselves as independently minded, however, for most of us, our minds have already made themselves up and know what they want us to do long before we try to think through the implications of the decisions we make.

To a large extent we completely identify with our minds. You're now probably thinking, "What do you mean my mind makes decisions on its own? *I* make the decisions. *I* think things through and come to an understanding as to what is right or wrong, and then act accordingly."

But think about it – who is arguing for the fact that you are independent of your mind? You are. Or at least your mind is.

Or are they the same thing? That is the real question.

Who is it that is doing the considering? Well, again your mind is, or at least another part of it is. The more we try to get away from our mind, the more entangled we become in the workings of our minds.

It is no wonder that we think we are our minds.

And most of us do.

If someone disagrees with us we tend to take it personally. People fight each other when they are offended. And by that we mean if our minds take offence at what someone else says about us.

If we think that someone is belittling us, or putting us down, our minds will think – "Hey that is me they are talking about. All those values and beliefs that I have amassed over the years, all that reputation that I have won are being belittled, and that it is not right. Therefore I must put a stop to it."

And who is thinking that – our minds are.

Our mind which has developed a sense of self-importance over the years, our mind which has come to certain conclusions about the sort of person we are, and the sort of person we are not. And if someone begins to challenge that – then we, that being "the royal we", which is really our minds, takes offence and decides that we must act.

Hence an argument, or a fight, or some sort of confrontation will occur so that the mind can reassert its supremacy.

And if it should lose that fight? Well rarely does the mind say – "Yes you were right about that and I was wrong." More often than not the mind will come up with a reason for why the other person was extra-wrong. That extra bit being shown by the illegitimate way in which the confrontation was conducted. So the mind becomes extra right. So:

Realisation number one: You are always in exactly the right place to be able to take the next step.

Realisation number two: You are not your mind.
But this is a tricky one, because look who is considering the question… your mind is. And you do not have another mind to use to consider it. You are trying to assess the mind using the mind, which is part of the problem of the monopoly.

If you wanted to assess the way a school was being run, you would not use the staff from the school to carry out the assessment; however objective they were being, they would still be blind to the mistakes that they were making at the school on a daily basis, because those self-same eyes that are blind to mistakes on a daily basis, will be blind to the mistakes even when they are trying to be objective.

If someone is colour blind, they will not be able to tell red from green, no matter how hard they try.

In the same way a mind that is blind to its own shortcomings will not be able to see those shortcomings, no matter how hard it tries.

And still I say – **You are not your mind.** There is more to you than all the thoughts and ideas and experiences that you have ever had.

"No," I can hear you say. "I am a person. I am my own person that uses my mind and comes to independent decisions about things."

Well, "person" is an interesting word. It comes from the Greek "Persona". The Persona was the mask that was worn by actors to represent the identity that they were representing on the stage. In Greek theatre all the actors wore such masks. It differentiated the actor from the identity they were playing.

The person that we think we are is really just the identity that our minds have created for ourselves over the years we have been alive.

It is the sum total of all the good and bad experiences we have ever had, and the decisions we have made about those good and bad experiences.

Gradually those experiences shape us, or at least they shape our minds and our minds tell us who we are. We are the sort of person who... Well you fill in the blanks. What sort of person are you?

Or who has your mind told you that you are?

This is why we must look a bit more at our minds.

A computer can never be spontaneous

Why not take a look at the way your mind works? Even if you think that there is nothing wrong with your mind, or you do not think that you are your mind, it will surely do no harm to look.

Begin with your rational mind. (There is obviously more to your mind than the rational bit – feelings, emotions, instincts are all a part of, or at least are affected by our minds.)

Here are a few instructions as to how to meet your mind.

Close your eyes. Not now, but after you have read this next paragraph or so.

Close your eyes and listen. Listen to that voice in your head. Even the voice that is saying, "What voice in my head?" Listen to it. Listen to the commentary that it makes about everything that is going on. About how stupid it is to be doing this. About how there is no point. About how you do not know what the point of all this is.

And when you have gone through that, listen to the mind noting things that are going on: That sound. That feeling in your body. That thought about what you could be doing right now. That thought about what you are going to do next.

OK, put the book down now, close your eyes and watch your mind at work.

That is your mind. Welcome to the world of "mindfulness": Watching your mind from a slight distance as it goes about its business.

You may have done it before. You may be aware of the concept of mindfulness, but it is a lifetime's work. It never stops, because your mind never stops. Your mind goes on all the time, from the moment you wake up to the moment you go to sleep. And your mind even carries on then, through dreams.

Watching your mind is simply another aspect of developing consciousness. Most of the time we are unconscious of the workings of our mind. We just take it for granted: Open the car door, start the engine, mirror, indicate, move out. It sounds like a driving lesson because a driving instructor wants you to be conscious of what is going on and instil a thought pattern that you then carry out unconsciously. But the thoughts are going on all the same.

Go downstairs, turn on the kettle, make the toast, turn on the radio, listen to music... it goes on all the time.

Sometimes we are challenged to think and we become aware of it: "Think, boy, the square of the hypotenuse..." And we think about our thinking to get the answer. But most of the time we are not conscious of it.

"I must buy some flowers for the party... and the drink... and get the cleaning equipment." This goes on all the time.

It is your rational mind at work, and a key aspect of developing your consciousness is being aware of that going on. Because that is what is often driving you to do things. Making those decisions that we have spoken about, deciding what to do and what not to do.

Most of the time all this goes on without us being aware of it; or of us having any awareness as to whether or not the actions we are taking are actually a good idea or a bad one.

By watching your mind at work you can become aware of those aspects of your minds that you want to support, and those you do not.

You might decide not to challenge someone to a fight over allegiance to a football team if you thought about it.

However, after eight pints of lager and a long night of activity, the mind probably does not have much consciousness of itself to make an informed decision about what it is going to do. The fist lashes out almost as if the mind had been completely bypassed. We even call it "mindless behaviour". Road rage is another example.

But closer to home, being aware of our minds might stop us

making too many decisions about someone by the kind of newspaper they read, the car they drive, or the music they listen to.

It might stop us buying that new pair of shoes, having that third drink, or sleeping with the wrong person. When we go on 'automatic' our minds take over and we do things that we do not always want to do.

You are not your mind.

Watching your mind will put you in control of your rational mind. It will enable you to develop greater awareness of everything that is going on around you and shape yourself as a person rather than living on automatic pilot.

Watching your mind is what allows you to develop your character, rather than have it emerge from the morass of random decisions that we spew out every day.

That is not to say that one should not be spontaneous. Spontaneity comes out of independence. A computer can never be spontaneous – it always makes its decisions based upon its programming. So it is with us: If we are not conscious of our minds, our spontaneity is just a function of being on automatic, and letting our minds dictate the next steps. If we are aware of our minds, we can make huge leaps outside the rationality of our thought; and within those leaps lies something of the nature of genius.

We always have the power within ourselves to change

We think that we are in control of our minds, but we are not.

Most of the times our mind is controlling us. It knows best.

It receives information from the senses and it assesses the information, and responds accordingly.

We think that we are making rational decisions, but, in actuality we are only acting on the options that we are being given by our mind.

It says, "Given this situation you have two options, A or B." You then think "Mmmmmm two options, if I do the first option then blaa blaa blaaa… and if I do the second option, well there is always blaa, blaa, blaa."

So we consider the options carefully and then decide what to do.

All very rational, all very in control of the information that the mind is giving you.

It is you that is making the decisions.

The thing that we fail to realise at the time is that there are not merely two options, there are dozens of them. The mind has automatically made all the calculations that it can think of and has come down to the two that it is happy to live with (i.e. the two that will enable it to maintain its survival in its current form).

Take the example of chocolate. You are in a supermarket at the checkout and you see a bar of chocolate. You are hungry. Your mind tells you that you have a choice – you either eat the chocolate, or you endure the pangs of hunger. You weigh up the alternatives and decide to buy the chocolate and eat it.

In fact there were many other alternatives: You could have turned back to the fruit counter and got an apple to deal with the hunger, or had a drink, or waited until you had left the checkout and had a snack at the restaurant.

Advertisers know this. They play to the mind in their advertising. Either buy this product with our brand name and be fashionable with your friends, or be seen as being out of touch. Everyone else has got high speed broadband; it stands to reason that you need it too. Drink this yoghurt and lose weight, or stay fat.

They are not the only options, but advertisers narrow them down to make us think that we are making informed choices.

The mind does the same thing. It automatically computes how we should respond to a situation, and then gives us only a couple of ways out.

Taking control of the mind is seeing that mechanism in action and slowing the process down so that you can assess all the options that are open to you and think creatively about how you are going to respond.

See if you can catch yourself making impulse choices today. Notice when you quickly decide something and act on it rather than weighing up the alternatives.

Bus or car to work?

What about walking, biking, car sharing, working from home, not going to work, making work come to you?

It is easy to think that this is ruining your spontaneity, but remember a computer is never spontaneous. It simply works things out faster. True spontaneity is watching the mind work, and then making a choice that is outside the way that you normally think.

"I'll walk my child to school and then get a lift from one of the parents I know who drives in to work near me."

A good definition of power is "the ability to act". When you have power you can act in any way that you want.

If you are Prime Minister, or the President of a country, your power is measured by your ability to act in any way that you want.

And so it is with us. Our power is defined in the same way.

An alcoholic is powerless because he is not able to get out of the cycle of drinking. It defines him and robs him of his ability to act independently.

His task is to free himself from his addiction.

All of us have a lot to learn from the 12 step programme that alcoholics use.

His first step is to admit that he is powerless over his addiction – that his life has become unmanageable. So he gradually recovers his power over his life by stopping drinking and by consciously making choices that put him in the driving seat of his life.

We have to do the same. We have to admit the extent to which our lives run on automatic: that we feel powerless to change our circumstances.

Instead we can come to realise that our power is *not* restricted by those circumstances, but only by the extent to which our mind is able to get a handle on the options that our circumstances give us.

Whereas a mind that is automatically computing will tell you that you cannot change anything. Change is possible.

By being fully conscious of what we are thinking and feeling, and knowing that we always have the power within ourselves to change – if not our circumstances, then at least the way that we think and feel about those circumstances.

Aged 10 – "It was like Mole talking to Ratty in the wild wood"

There is one thing that will almost certainly guarantee you being bullied at school, and that is being fat.

And if you are fat with no concept of love, and no idea of how to make proper relationships, and consequently always being in trouble, then it is as good as being handed "The Black Spot". You're dead.

I was immediately marked out as a troublemaker, or to be less glamorous, "out of control".

I was forced to put my desk at the front of the class, behind the teacher and with the edge touching the wall next to the blackboard, so I could not influence others.

Fights regularly broke out between classes. I can remember someone stabbing me in the arm with a biro, so I stabbed him in the back with a pencil. My mail from home was stolen and opened; I was punched, kicked, called all the fat names you can think of, and reduced to misery.

We were also regularly terrorised by the older boys.

One night I was in the gym with a class of 12 year olds.

I was quickly put on a bench and beaten. As I fell off I hit my head on the floor and blacked out. I can remember seeing a master come in the door as I lifted my head out of a sticky pool of my own blood.

You were never left alone. From mealtimes, to classes, to breaks, there were always opportunities for fights or name calling.

"You're fat, so why should you play?"

"I bet you stole those, give them to me."

I can remember one teacher telling me I had done a particularly good piece of work, but he could not understand why the writing was smudged in the middle of the page. I could not tell him that it was because I had been hit from behind at random in the middle of prep, and had cried into my exercise book.

At night, in the long 30 bed dormitories, when the lights were put out, boys would go from bed to bed, inviting other boys to wank them off.

Masters would catch boys talking and would take them off to be beaten.

Most of the time they were beaten with a slipper, so severely that the whole of the buttocks came up in red weals.

When I went home at the holidays it was impossible to tell my mother what had been happening. She asked me why all the cuffs of my jerseys had been chewed away. I could not tell her that it was the only relief I got when I was crying.

It never occurred to me to run away.

Eventually my reports became so bad, and my work suffered so much that I was asked to go and see the headmaster.

We sat opposite each other on two chairs. He asked me what was wrong.

I couldn't tell him. You can't as a child; it just won't come out. It is a cross between the fear of telling tales, and that fact that adults cannot understand because they live in a different world. You just keep it bottled up.

"Can you tell me what the matter is?" he asked again.

I could feel the confusion welling up within me. I did not know what to say or how to say it. He began to see my distress. He came over to my chair and took me in his arms, sitting me down on his knee.

"What's that matter, old chap?" he said in a voice that I had never before heard from a man. It was like Mole talking to Ratty in the wild wood about his home. And a huge sob came right up from the deepest place within me and burst upon his shoulder. Then another, and then another.

As he held me, and the sobs came, I could smell the pipe smoke on his clothes, and feel the coarseness of his jacket. I had never been held by a man before and it opened up a flood of emotion that wracked my body with sobs.

The headmaster just held me – he knew what to do. I carried on until the last convulsions pulled themselves out of my body, and I lay against him, at peace.

He probably saved my life, my sanity at least.

However, I was never going to get into such a place again. I made a mental note that from that time on I was not going to be at the effect of my emotions. I was not going to be subject to others. I was going to make my own way.

And so I did.

I began to learn to read a roomful of people as if they were enemy warships; and if they even started to train their guns on me, I made sure I created a diversion.

I became the life and soul of the class (although still a pretty pathetic one). I made jokes, was constantly accused by masters of being "immature" and of "showing off", but the bullying began to stop. And so did the crying.

I decided that I was not going to be reduced to tears again.

That no longer would I be left snivelling in the classroom while others laughed.

If anything, others would do the snivelling.

I would never cry again.
And, to this day, I have not.

The purpose of the mind is to survive

The purpose of the mind is to survive.

And by that I do not mean just that the purpose of the mind is to keep us alive; however, that is very much a part of it.

No, the purpose of the mind is *its* survival, and that generally coincides with the survival of us as individuals, but there is a distinction. The mind will often prefer to be right, than to allow the person that inhabits it to survive.

Like HAL, the computer in the film *2001: A Space Odyssey*, the mind will do everything that it can to enable it to survive in a form that it thinks it should occupy.

Obviously it is designed to keep us alive. In Stone Age time it instinctively acted with information from the senses to keep us away from the danger of the hairy mammoth, and to make sure that we had enough food to keep us alive. But nowadays it tends to "over-survive".

Which is why issues of respect are so important to people. Some of us will be willing to fight over the smallest of issues if our minds do not get the respect we have become accustomed to expect from others.

In the East the idea of "losing face" can lead people to kill themselves in order to preserve the honour that they have developed over their lives.

I do not fully understand the implications of such actions; however, they do illustrate an example of when the survival of the mind does not always coincide with the survival of the individual.

It happens when we think that we are our minds, and our minds tell us that if we do not follow through on this or that behaviour, we will be as good as dead.

And when minds associate with other minds and think that they are part of a greater mind, again it can lead to death – as when we associate ourselves with the mind that is our country, or the mind that is our religion. That "controlling mind" then creates a greater good that makes it decide that death is preferable to letting that conceptualisation of goodness be eradicated.

I am not saying that this is right or wrong; I am just saying that it happens, and then the mind sees being right as more important than its death.

The purpose of the mind is to survive; however, the survival of the mind, in its own terms, does not mean to say that we as individuals will survive. So we have to be aware of that.

Because **we are not our minds.**

So we have to watch our minds to make sure that the bit that it is enabling it to survive is the bit that we want to have survive.

We do not want to get caught up in a heightened emotionalism that robs us of our rational faculties, like Nazi Germany – an example of the rational mind becoming irrational.

Nor, on the other hand, do we want to get run over by a bus, so we have to pay attention to what the mind is telling us about the big red thing that is travelling towards us at high speed and hear that it says we need to get out of the way *fast.*

The problem is that the mind makes decisions in the blink of an eye, and those decisions are not always the right ones.

Malcolm Gladwell, the writer who came up with the idea of "the tipping point", has written a book called *Blink.*

It's a book about rapid cognition, about the kind of thinking that happens in a blink of an eye. When you meet someone for the first time, or walk into a house you are thinking of buying, or read the first few sentences of a book, your mind takes about two seconds to jump to a series of conclusions.

One of the stories he tells in *Blink* is about the Emergency

Room doctors at Cook County Hospital in Chicago. That's the big public hospital in Chicago, and a few years ago they changed the way they diagnosed heart attacks. They instructed their doctors to gather *less* information on their patients: they encouraged them to zero in on just a few critical pieces of information about patients suffering from chest pain – like blood pressure and the ECG – while ignoring everything else, like the patient's age and weight and medical history. Taking information away from the mind and stopping it making automatic calculations based upon what the person looks like, both in the flesh and on paper. Instead it forced clinicians to concentrate on a small number of highly relevant pieces of information, and do one specific calculation.

And what happened? Cook County is now one of the best places in the United States at diagnosing chest pain.

The mind often jumps to conclusions that are not always right.

Persistent unwanted conditions

So, where does the mind go wrong, and what can we do about it?

The mind goes wrong when it processes information and comes out with a picture of reality that is incorrect.

Most of us live with an incorrect picture of reality most of the time. We just settle for one that seems to work.

Just as civilisation settled for the idea that the world was flat until Galileo came along, so we develop our own view of life that serves as a working hypothesis, until something comes along and proves it wrong.

We might think that all strangers are untrustworthy. Our parents taught us never to talk to strangers, we hear examples of people who are robbed or ripped off by strangers, and so it pretty much works to assume that all strangers are untrustworthy, at least until proven otherwise.

Now this is obviously not true, but as a way of looking at life it has merit. We will not fall into any traps and it makes us wary at times when we might expect trouble.

And yet it is not true.

The trouble is that we have millions of these "working hypotheses" that we use every day to navigate our ways through life, and we gradually come to believe the overall picture they paint about the way life is.

We learn from our experiences, and learn to make decisions about our life that may or may not be true.

We may have come from a family that did not show much physical love. We then start to get the idea that no one expresses love in a physical way. We do not show affection ourselves, nor do we look for affection from others. Gradually we develop a view of life that simply does not include physical affection. We seek out people who live life the same way, and everything we believe about the nature of physical affection is confirmed in them. And so we see life in a certain way that does not include an aspect that many others feel is vital to life.

What happens is that some of the sensory receptors in our brain fail to operate. In this case those receptors relate to physical affection. As these receptors are failing, the overall picture of the nature of reality is skewed. And so we gradually build up a reality of life that does not include physical affection.

The problem comes when we find that we are developing other needs to compensate for the release that physical affection brings. We might become stern and controlling, thinking that this is the only way to create co-operation. We might begin to drink alcohol to replace the feelings that physical affection brings. We might begin to use sex as a way of getting the release that we would normally get through gentler, more regular physical contact. We might develop a passion for stamp collecting – pouring all our frustration into creating the perfect stamp collection, and gaining satisfaction from that.

However we develop, our reality has been affected by that lack of physicality. We think that this is the way life is; that others experience life in the same way.

We might even begin to look down on people who demonstrate any overt physical affection as being weak, or soft, or even unnatural. What we really mean is that it is not natural to us, and therefore we make a sweeping judgement as to what should be natural for others.

Our reality becomes one without physical affection, and our life becomes about compensating for that lack.

Eventually, after many years, if we are able to get some ability to self-reflect we begin to ask ourselves why it is that others seem to have relationships that run smoothly, and yet we lurch from one crisis to another, using whatever is at hand (drink, drugs or sex) to steady the ship. We also begin to wonder why it is that whoever we date, they always turn out to be the same sort of person – generally people who are not interested in physical affection.

We end up with what is called a persistent unwanted condition.

It does not have to be about physical affection, it could be anything:

The inability to follow something through to the end because you think you will always fail.
The inability to trust people fully.
A tendency towards anger and physical violence.
Always ending up being ignored.
Codependency.
....

Fill in the gap for your life.

In each case it comes about through a misunderstanding of the nature of reality. A shutting down of our senses, leading to a warped view of reality, which then develops a coping mechanism to create balance in an unbalanced world.

We come to believe that the earth is flat, and construct our lives accordingly.

The trick is to develop our consciousness to see these persistent unwanted conditions for what they are – a response to a warped view of life.

Aged 19 – "Then it was the turn of the testicles"

I know a little of what it takes to become a concentration camp guard.

There were eighty-four thousand acres of Australian outback, thirty-four thousand sheep, two thousand cattle and seven of us. We controlled the animals through fear and the knife.

Early on in the trip we were mustering a heard of two thousand sheep across a paddock. Most of the sheep were mature merinos, bred for their wool.

I spotted at the side of the heard a tiny lamb, no more than a foot long, born out of season and trying to keep up with its mother. Eventually it gave up and flopped down on the ground, exhausted.

I picked it up and gingerly took it to one of the senior jackeroos (sheep cowboys).

He took the lamb from me, held it by its hind legs, dashed its head against a nearby tree and threw the bloody body into the bush. "It would never have lived anyway," he said over his shoulder as he walked away. So began my education into the ways of the outback.

It was the mosquitoes that were the worst. As big as a ten pence piece they were able to bite their way through a pair of jeans, and in the morning all the metal fences were black with them as they tried to suck moisture from the condensation. I wore two pairs of jeans and a para smock in 100 degrees of heat, just to keep them off. At night I had a fan trained on my face all the time to stop them biting – mosquito nets did not seem to exist.

Frogs lived in the lavatory bowls and in the cistern above your head. When you flushed, they slipped down from under the rim where they lived to keep cool.

One afternoon we brought in 1500 young male sheep.

Each in turn was picked up. You lifted the sheep so that its back rested on your chest, and supported its weight by holding its two hind legs, one in each hand.

You then held the legs open, exposing the tail and the two large balls.

Another jackeroo stood in front of you with a knife.

First they lifted the tail and with one swift movement severed it from the body. Blood squirted as if from a water pistol. Then it was the turn of the testicles. You lifted them by the skin of the scrotum which you held between your thumb and forefinger. You then made a cut straight through the sack just in front of your thumb. Dropping the small piece of sack you turned the knife round, revealing a hook. This was placed at the base of the scrotum, and then, one at a time, you pulled the balls – out and up.

They looked like bloody fleshy eggs with strings coming off them. As you threw them on the ground the dogs rushed forward for the tasty snack. The stringy bits had to come out, otherwise there was a chance that the sheep would continue to behave like a male, rather than a eunuch. If you left the tubes in the animal it was said to be "cut proud".

We castrated and tailed 1500 sheep that afternoon.

For breakfast, lunch and supper we ate mutton.

The meat came from a particular flock known as "The Killers".

Every so often one was taken and prepared.

I was to go over to learn how to do it.

They gave you a knife. The idea was to get the sheep on its side, then put your knee on its stomach so that it could not move. You then held back its head with one hand and thrust the point of the knife into the other, cutting outward and slitting its throat from ear to ear. You then pushed the head back hard on to the body, thereby breaking the neck. Blood went everywhere.

Every evening the seven of us came together for a meal in the dining room of the station. I sat at the side of the table with the station manager's wife, Mrs Adams, on my left at the head of the table. Opposite her was Mr Adams, and three other jackeroos at the sides.

This one particular evening we all stopped eating as we heard a peculiar buzzing noise.

Coming into sight, above Mr Adams' head, flew a giant cockroach. We all sat open mouthed and watched it as it made its way over Mr Adams and began to fly the length of the table.

Mrs Adams at the other end was also open-mouthed, but not quite fast enough.

The insect flew, almost in slow motion, down the length of the table and directly into her mouth. Mrs Adams' lips then automatically closed over the creature, leaving its back legs protruding from her mouth.

We all sat stunned and watched the little legs moving up and down. Mrs Adams seemed paralysed and remained completely motionless. I cannot remember what happened next as the whole moment has become frozen in time.

Gradually, over the months I became inured to the plight of the sheep, the killing and maiming becoming as everyday as eating and sleeping.

By the end I no longer saw it. In fact when I was asked by a new jackeroo what to do about a sheep that had got its foot stuck in a

plank in the sheds, I said, "Cut it off."
I think I was only joking.

What is real for us is what our senses tell us and what we observe

Sogyal Rinpoche in his version of the Tibetan Book of Living and Dying[3] has a poem by Portia Nelson that perfectly illustrates the dilemma that we face with persistent unwanted conditions, and how we get out of them.

Autobiography in 5 Chapters

1. I walk down the street.
There is a deep hole in the pavement.
I fall in.
I am lost… I am hopeless.
It isn't my fault.
It takes forever to find a way out.

2. I walk down the same street.
There is a deep hole in the pavement.
I pretend I don't see it.
I fall in again.
I can't believe I'm in the same place.
But it isn't my fault.
It still takes a long time to get out.

3. I walk down the same street.
There is a deep hole in the pavement.
I see it is there.
I still fall in… it's a habit.
My eyes are open.
I know where I am.

It is my fault.
I get out immediately.

4. I walk down the same street.
There is a deep hole in the pavement.
I walk around it.

5. I walk down another street.

It takes us so long to get it because the mind always wants to be right about the way that it sees life.

There is an argument that can be put forward that monkey brains are actually more adaptable than human brains.

Put a monkey in a cage with two buttons. If the monkey presses the first button he gets a grape. If he presses the other button he gets an electric shock.

Very soon the monkey learns which button gives him the grape and which the electric shock and he always gets the grape.

If, however, you swap the buttons over after a short period of time so that the button that gave the grape now gives the electric shock, the monkey first shows surprise and confusion, but after only a relatively short space of time adapts again and learns which button will deliver the grape.

With human beings it is more complicated.

The human mind will quickly work out which button to push to get the grape. However, if you swap them over the mind will often stick with the same button.

It will say, "I know from my past experience that when I press this button I got the grape, so I will continue to press it."

After a while it says to itself, "I know I am getting an electric shock at the moment, but that is the price I have to pay to eventually get the grape." This may go on for years until the idea of the grape becomes a distant memory. The mind now says, "The electric shock is good because it reminds us what grapes taste like. We suffer because we know that we will eventually get the grape, either in this life or the next." Eventually the human passes "the ritual of the electric shock" on to the next generation.

That generation is so far removed from the grape that it begins to see that the electric shock itself brings value because it reminds us that we are alive. It has its own medicinal properties, as well as reminding us of the grape.

And so the next generation gradually forms "The Order of the Grape" that includes the ritual of the electric shock. The grape becomes the promise of life in this world, or the next, and the shock becomes the way we connect with the grape.

You see the way it goes. We human beings are so complicated.

Persistent unwanted conditions come from a misapprehension of the nature of reality, and our task in developing consciousness is to begin to establish the true nature of that reality.

So far we have simply begun to look at what we need to become more conscious of – our senses, our thoughts, the way our mind works. By following this path we acknowledge reality through our experience, rather than as what we have come to *think* of as reality. In this way we begin to see what is actually real for us.

Because of the way we live our lives, most of us have developed ideas about the way life works, our worldview, and this largely comes from others.

Other people work out theories, write them down in books, and then our mind either agrees or disagrees with them, depending on what decisions it has made about life in the past.

If it agrees with the ideas, it adopts them as a part of its own belief system and so builds up a reality. This is very different from actually watching the reality that we live through by noticing our senses, noticing the way we think, noticing the way the mind works, and noticing how we respond to our minds.

That is our reality, as opposed to our thoughts about reality.

What is real for us is what our senses tell us and what we observe.

This is the beginning of reality and will lead us to enlightenment. For enlightenment is actually the ability to perceive the true nature of reality.

The power to determine the nature of your reality still lies in your own hands

So how come we develop this taste for unreality? What stopped us trusting our own senses and our own thoughts as a way of working out what is going on?

It starts at a very early age.

When we are very little we think that we are perfect and that life is perfect. We do not see imperfection anywhere. Our parents coo over us and tell us that they love us, whatever we do, including puking up over them and pooing whenever and wherever we like.

We can do no wrong.

Then suddenly, one day, probably at about the age of two, you pick up a crayon and see this huge expanse of whiteness in front of you. Mummy and daddy always like the pictures that you draw, saying how great they always are, so you decide to do a huge picture for them.

You cover the white space in all the colours that you have, making a fabulously creative design.

But when you fetch mummy and show her what you have done, she reacts with fury. "How could you be so naughty," she shouts, "drawing all over the wall." She gets daddy and both of them make a lot of noise which seems to be directed at you.

And so you have the first dawning realisation that things are not all as they should be. That, horror of horrors, you have done something that is not perfect.

In fact it is more than that. You have the terrible realisation that you are not perfect.

You are not perfect, and the world is not perfect.

And so you think, or rationalise as only two year olds can, and you come up with the next basic question:

"If I am not perfect, what must I do to be perfect?"

It is logical. You were perfect, now you are not, so how do you go back to perfection? And the answer is there, right in front of you in the shape of your parents.

They told you that you are not perfect. Therefore they must tell you how to be perfect. And so you make the fateful decision that will stay with you for the rest of your life:

You do what you think they will approve of.

You begin to seek approval. You do not get it right every time. In fact sometimes you are so angry about things that you wilfully go against their approval (especially in adolescence). But basically you begin to see yourself in terms of the way others see you. You want to please others, because then they are nice to you and life works better.

And so corruption sets in. You continually try to second guess what you ought to do in life; not using your own experience, but looking to the experience of others.

You give away the one real power that you have, the power to act on your life experiences.

Over the years you give away power to friends (peer pressure), teachers, religions, groups, governments, gurus; in fact anyone who can make a case for knowing more about life than you do.

Now obviously in many cases it is appropriate to give away such power. Your education depends upon it. Bosses have a right to it. Governments demand it, and will exert consequences if you do not follow the rules they lay down.

And yet you still have the ultimate responsibility for deciding about the way you live your life – the way you decide on the nature of the reality that you live within. But, in many cases you give that away too.

And so you are left feeling helpless. Not knowing where to start if you want to challenge anything. You feel that others always know more about life than you do. They are always better read, better travelled, have more money, success or power, and generally leave you with the feeling of, "What do I know anyway?"

Some people make it their business to ensure that you feel "less than". Class systems and caste systems are ways that generations of families have developed to make sure that their own kind stay on top, and the rest of us feel that it is not worth competing because we are "less than".

So in the end you give up trying, get on that treadmill and keep peddling in the hope that it will at least get you somewhere. And, of course, it never does because the treadmill is fixed firmly to the ground. The whole reality is an illusion.

But, you still have that power in your own hands, if you would but use it. As the Dictionary of Psychology said about consciousness, *"Nothing worth reading has been written about it."* In other words, the power to determine the nature of your reality still lies in your own hands. Not only that, but the power to determine how to respond to that reality also lies with you. And so you can determine your life, or at least how you experience and interpret it.

Aged 24 – "We were to each have our moment alone with the Pope"

I had never seen a dead body before, nor a Pope, so to see both at the same time was too good to miss.

I was looking for a holiday. So when I saw that the Pope had died and was going to be lying in state in Rome, I had my destination.

*Rome was hot and dusty and I ended up in a run-down hotel
somewhere near the centre of the city. Wooden floors with worn
rugs; a spongy mattress with slightly damp sheets.*

*The action was at St Peter's Square with the dead Pope lying in
state in the Basilica. This was the one that died very soon after
being elected, so the rumour was that he had been murdered.
Thousands of people milled around the square. It looked like it
does when the Pope speaks from that window high above the
square. Except he was dead.*

*What I hadn't bargained for was an eight hour queue to see the
body.*

*Queue jumping is an art. Fail at it and you risk being vilified
and humiliated by everyone who can see that you have barged in.
The trick is to minimise the number of people that see you barge.
The way you do that is to choose a place where the queue turns
a corner at a right angle by a wall – or some other obstacle.*

*Edge your way forward to the place in the queue just in front of
the corner, so that there are only a couple of people who are
between you and the corner. Behind them the queue then disap-
pears at the right angle.*

*At some point those people who you go in front of will notice
that you have barged in. They will become indignant and you
immediately apologise profusely, and allow those in the queue to
push you back behind them, around the corner.*

*The people at the other side of the corner have not seen you barge
in, they have only seen the people in front of you push past you,
and so, in their eyes, you are the victim, and they make no move
to eject you. You are therefore accepted in the queue as of right.*

*I barged the queue at St Peter's Basilica just before the doors,
and was soon making my way up the nave into the vast church.
We shuffled our way forward in single file.*

*About 150 yards ahead was the dais, upon which the Pope's body
lay, uncovered and with his face available for all to see.*

Television cameras were in fixed positions everywhere, carrying the event live on Italian television, and recording highlights that would go all around the world. It was a global event.

All the way up the nave stood the Vatican Guard with their colourful outfits and swords, or pikes, held in reverse, with their points to the floor.

Four guards stood above the four corners of the dais on elevated platforms, looking down upon the ex-Pope.

We shuffled our way up the aisle.

As we got close to the front I noticed that there was a red cord with a silver hook at the end, like those used to control nightclub queues. We were to each have our moment alone with the Pope. As the next person came along, so the guard raised the chord and that person made their way along a narrowly roped-off corridor next to the dais. You were encouraged to keep moving, and after the dais another chord was lifted so that you could leave.

There was anticipation all around as people prepared for their audience with the Pope. Albeit one that had already gone to meet his maker.

I felt it too; the global spectacle, the cameras, the guards, all the people and the Pope. I began to realise that, if only just for a moment, I was going to be at the very centre of all this activity. For just that moment it was going to be me and the Pope, with thousands of people all around and the world watching, with cameras pointing in my direction.

This could be my moment, "the" moment; my chance for world fame.

I began to see all the headlines around the world: "British man desecrates the Pope's body." The scandal, the interest, crowds of people pointing cameras in my direction. Me being the story.

Just as I was thinking this the red chord was lifted and I was there. Just me, the Pope and the cameras. I could feel panic fighting in my stomach. It was now or never.

I looked towards the yellow waxy face, the two hands forced, presumably stitched, together in a position of prayer, The small

feet in pointy shoes. Everything slowed down. I... lifted... my...
hands... my legs... took... me... forward and suddenly the rope
at the other side was up and I was out.
I collapsed forward into a pew, fighting for my breath and
attempting to regain my composure as if profoundly moved by
my time with the holiest man on earth.
Years later I still remember that feeling – the sweetness of the
thought of all that attention, the attractiveness of the swift
action that would both make and unmake my life for ever. I still
feel tempted on occasions. But never so strongly as on that day
in Rome.

Move from looking at the content of our consciousness, to the nature of that consciousness

Someone once said that the road to enlightenment is paved with questions not answers.

The moment you get an answer you stop. It is the questions that lead you on.

It is tempting to say that the answer to the meaning of life lies in the simple observation of what is so: Of feeling the feelings that we feel. Of thinking the thoughts that we think. Of consciously making the decisions that we make.

The problem is that this does not seem to get us anywhere. It just takes us round in circles. Not only that, but it is probably worth saying at this point that this, in itself, is a lifetime's work.

You wake up in the morning and you think, "Right, I am going to observe my thoughts all day today," you pull the covers off (consciously realising that you are doing it while you are doing it) throw your legs out of bed, begin to walk (consciously) to the bathroom, and when you get in there you notice that your husband has left the top off the toothpaste tube again. How many times have you told him about that? What will it take for him to… and then you have lost it.

At lunchtime you remember that you had decided to be conscious of your thoughts all day; and you make a mental note of your failure, and decide to start again tomorrow.

For me it is like giving up smoking.

It took me five years to give up, and it was a major battle with my mind (as is giving up any addiction).

It got so bad that I would give up smoking for life in the morning, and find myself having a cigarette at lunchtime.

Here's an example of how tricky our minds can be:

I thought that the best way to give up smoking for good was to go to someone that I really respected, and make a solemn agreement with them that I was going to give up smoking, and if I had another cigarette, whenever that was, I would pay them £1,000.

All went well for a few months. Then one evening I felt the pressure to have a fag. It had been a rough day, there was a beer in front of me and people around me. I definitely wanted a smoke.

My mind frantically raced for a solution. Up and down all the possibilities like a rat in a cage. And then, as the mind always does, it found the cheese. Bingo! I know what I'll do, I'll have a cigarette, and I won't pay my friend the £1,000 I owe him. What's he going to do about it anyway? Nothing.

So I had the cigarette and didn't pay my friend. My mind won again.

And so it is with observing our minds. We always fail (unlike with giving up smoking which I eventually managed). The pressures of life always take us out of that observation and into whatever crisis we find ourselves in. It is inevitable.

How could we continually look at our thoughts anyway? We'd go mad. And what is the point of just feeling our feelings if it doesn't get us anywhere?

Much better to go out there and do something. Make

something happen. Change the world, or if not that, at least make some money.

It was Einstein who said that, "No problem can be solved from the same level of consciousness that created it."

And so it is with us. Even though we are aware of our feelings, of our thoughts, of our decisions, it is not going to make the blindest bit of difference to our lives unless we can take a step back and look at life from another level of consciousness.

Up to now all we have been talking about is our observation of our own consciousness.

That in itself is a major step forward.

In fact if you are able to feel those feelings when you feel them, and think those thoughts when you think them, you will probably have a much greater grasp of what is real than most people that you meet on the street.

The problem is that we have to do more than that. Some say that 98% of our thoughts are useless anyway: Stupid observations about what is going on, people we see, sex, judgements, what ifs, plans that will never happen, and plans that will. All of it going round and round and round.

We do not observe our thoughts and feelings in order to learn from the things that we are thinking and feeling.

We observe our thoughts and feelings to realise that we are not them.

You are not your mind (actually, that feels like a relief now, doesn't it?). Nor are you your feelings. They happen within you. The very fact you can observe them means that you can be outside them. (And I know you can say that this is just the mind observing the mind, but there is nothing wrong with that – we have been given our minds, so we might as well use them, as opposed to being used *by* them.)

The fact that we can observe our consciousness means that we can move from looking at the *content* of our consciousness to the *nature* of that consciousness.

The nature of consciousness

This is the second major leap. The first leap was to be aware of what is going on in our consciousness. The second is to be aware of consciousness itself.

It is the difference between observing the contents of our minds and seeing the actual workings of the mind, the context.

It is quite a complicated leap. The Dalai Lama describes it very well in his book *The Good Heart*.[4] He says:

> "The nature of consciousness... is such that it is not at all material; it has no material form or shape or colour whatsoever. As such, it is not quantifiable in scientific terms, and it thus does not lend itself to current scientific investigation. Instead of having some material nature, consciousness is by nature "mere experience" or "mere awareness".
>
> When I say: "I know," or "I'm aware," there seems to be an agent "I" who engages in the activity of knowing or being aware; but what we mean by consciousness is that capacity in dependence upon which knows or is aware.
>
> It is, in other words, the activity or process of knowing itself, and, as such, it is "mere awareness"....
>
> This is because, generally speaking, we associate it (consciousness) with an external object or with a pleasant or unpleasant sensation. That is, whether we are thinking conceptually or simply having a sensory experience, awareness itself arises with the form or appearance of an object, and as a result, we usually do not recognise it as "mere awareness"... In short, in our ordinary experience consciousness becomes caught up with the dualistic appearances of "object" and "subject"...
>
> So... if you are able to put a stop to... the turbulence within the mind — the conceptual thought processes and thought patterns chasing after sensory experiences — you can begin to perceive the deeper level.

If you are totally withdrawn, that does not help in this process. You must maintain an alertness and gradually stop the fluctuations of thought and sensory experiences within your mind.

Then it is possible to have a glimpse of the nature of the mind.

Initially, when you first experience this nature, you experience it as only a type of vacuity. But it is possible, through practice, to extend that period.

And then the nature of mind, this clarity and cognizance, will become more and more apparent. This is how it is possible to recognise the nature of consciousness in contrast to the consciousness that is linked to physical reality."

It is complicated, but it is also good to get it from the horse's mouth. My understanding is that this next step in developing consciousness is to realise that this thing that we call "consciousness", is *not* all that stuff that we see and hear and feel in our lives. Those things are merely the objects that our consciousness perceives around us. Consciousness itself is the *capacity* that we have to see and hear and feel those things. And it is possible to be conscious of the capacity we have to see, as well as all the things we see.

Take the example of a digital camera.

The camera is not the pictures that it takes. It is a mechanism by which we can take pictures and then see them.

So our consciousness is not the things that we perceive; it is the capacity that we have that enables us to see and perceive.

Most of our lives we are so bound up with responding to our senses – being hungry, or thirsty, needing a pee, or wanting sex, or wanting that car or that job or whatever, such that our minds do not have any consciousness on that aspect that is enabling it to function.

It is preoccupied with sorting its way through the maze of life. Working out which way to go, and how to go about getting there.

But by stopping… and watching those senses and those thoughts taking place… and by considering the fact that there is something that is doing the thinking and sensing and deciding, we begin to become aware of the machine that is doing all the actions.

The next step is becoming more and more aware of that.

Of becoming aware of the length and breadth, and height of that capacity.

The Dalai Lama says that the way to do this is to become less thrown about by the senses: *Noticing* that your senses are telling you that you want a peanut butter sandwich, but just noting it rather than rushing off to get one.

Or noticing that you want to argue with something that a friend says, rather than actually launching into an argument.

This enables us to slow down the perceived pace of our lives and *"gradually stop the fluctuations of thought and sensory experiences within your mind."*

The deliberate practice of actually doing that is what is called meditation, and there are various things that people do to make that come about in a formal way, but we will come back to that later on.

The Dalai Lama goes on to say that when we first begin to get a sense of this it seems like a kind of emptiness, or vacuity. But, as we get used to it, we gradually become aware of the realm of consciousness that we have at our disposal.

That there is a vast capacity available for us to use in becoming more conscious of the true nature of our reality. And that, at the moment, we are only using a tiny bit of it.

Aged 25 – "Everyone else thought it was wonderful"

There were 9 of us, with 26 Sherpas and porters. They carried everything, including a dining room table from which we ate every evening.

The day began at 5.30am when we were awoken in our tents by a Sherpa putting a metal bowl of hot water through the flaps. We crawled out and into the early morning mist of the Himalayas.

After washing there was a cry of, "Tee leddy," which indicated that the tea had brewed and was ready for drinking.

While we sipped the porters took down our tents and packed up the whole camp. We watched as they put everything on their backs and strode out towards the mountains.

We finished our tea, picked up our staffs that had been given to us to help us on the rocky terrain, and followed the men out of the camp.

We generally walked for about 5 hours. The entire trek would take 17 days and cover 125 miles up 14,000 feet of the Jugal Himal mountain range. It was a circular walk so that, if someone fell ill, one of the Sherpas would be made to run back to Kathmandu to summon the helicopter to come to our rescue.

As we came across mountain villages we opened our first aid kits, and Richard, the doctor, held a surgery. The only time we ever sent for help was when we discovered cholera in a villager.

At about 11 we caught up with the porters who had already laid out rugs for us to lie on and made lunch. As we ate, the porters set off once again.

Our leader was Edward Montagu, Lord Montagu of Beaulieu, off to see the rhododendrons that cover the slopes of the Himalayas in April.

The afternoon march ended at about 5 when we walked into our camp, which the porters had already pitched for us.

We fell exhaustedly into our tents while supper was prepared.

Ruth, one of the women on the trek, was not eating with us as she had adopted the only animal that the Sherpas had brought with them, a kid goat.

This followed us for three days and then disappeared.

After supper on the fourth day Ruth asked the head Sherpa what had happened to the goat.

"You have just eaten it," the Sherpa replied.

Ruth did not speak to anyone for two days.

I had never been so out in the wilderness before and I hated it. I counted down the days till we got back. 15, 14, 13, 12... Pooing in the outdoors, endless walking uphill. The altitude, the cold above the snow line. I dreamt of hot baths and cool towels. Everyone else thought it was wonderful. And when we had one day off from walking, they even chose to visit a glacier – more walking.

I stayed in my tent and rested.

But there was no getting away from it. You really had to be there. Moment by moment, step by step, day by day.

And only the comfort of the thought of a smoke at the end of the day to keep me going.

The Sherpas and porters were always up for a laugh. It never entered my head that theirs was the real pain on the trip. We just took them for granted.

And then, one day we emerged at the top of the particular mountain we had been travelling up. We pitched camp, or rather the porters did, on the side of the mountain, above the cloud line looking across at a line of peaks that stretched out into the sky.

That night the moon rose high in the sky flooding everything with its milky weak light.

There we were, and there it was. A sea of cloud beneath us, and these huge peaks emerging like icebergs across to the horizon in front of us. It was wonderful.

It was full of wonder. I was full of wonder.

Gone were my cynical comments. My sarcastic asides. My desire for comfort. This was another world to my own. It left the struggles and strains of London life as a tree leaves the ants at its

base and soars to the sky. I had never seen such a sight as this.
All you could say was WOW, WOW and thrice WOW.
My spirit seemed to rise to meet my soul, and take it somewhere
new. Somewhere that would change it forever.
It had seen an inexpressible sight, one that it would never forget.
I reached for a fag and lit up.
In the end I did not think that the trip had changed me. It was
my mother who told me, much later, that she knew something
was different when I met her in London a few weeks later, still
wearing Indian clothes and claiming to be vegetarian.

Consciously control yourself to observe the mind

Another way of looking at the nature of the mind, as opposed to its contents, is to see it as a supercharger in a car engine.

You drive along going from one gear to another. Incidentally, one of the things we use to change gear in our lives is our emotions.

The word emotion comes from two Latin words *movere* (to move) and *ex* (out of): to move out of. Our emotions enable us to move from one experience to another.

When someone close to us dies we feel sad. That sadness enables us to adjust to the change in our reality of the person not being there. We cry, we mourn, and we expend energy.

After a while, we can look back and put the loss within the greater context of our life experience.

How long that takes obviously depends on how deeply the loss has changed the landscape of our lives. The loss of a loved one can take years to adapt to.

(Incidentally one can get trapped on the emotional transition, not being able or willing to move on, because the strong emotion that we experience in some way keeps us close to the person that we have lost, and therefore we do not want to let it go. But in general the purpose of emotion is to move us on.)

And so we drive through our lives changing gear as we navigate our way to our destination, using our mind as the engine.

The supercharge element is the capacity to see that we have yet another gear that we can move into. One that enables us to completely disengage from the engine of the mind, and engage another supercharged engine that will add a huge amount of power to the workings of our mind.

By and large our minds are in control. We sense, we appraise, and we act. We then re-sense, re-appraise, and re-act. And so it goes on.

But imagine that you are able to go into a kind of neutral gear. One where the mind (the engine) is still turning over, but we are not forced to do what it says.

Let's try it.

Find an image or fabric or wallpaper with some sort of pattern in it.

Gaze at the image from a distance without blinking.

As you do so you will notice that the pattern begins to go out of focus. Try not to refocus your eyes. Instead let the pattern swim in front of you. Your mind will want to make you focus, because it always wants to get a picture of what is going on out there so that it can sense, assess and react.

Consciously do not let it focus. Consciously let the image swim in front of you. Gradually you will begin to see the picture seem to move of its own accord.

Let go of what your mind is trying to make of the image, and let the image make itself in your mind.

Now, of course the image is not moving; however, your mind cannot deal with the image being out of focus, so, like a computer, it is desperately trying to join up the dots and make an image that is can assess and react to. Hence the image moves.

The process should take about 5 minutes.

Try it now. Do not press into focus – try to gaze at it – try not to blink – but don't make the image, let the image make itself.

Did you see movement? Of course the image did not actually move. But the key thing is to disengage your mind and stop it telling you what to do. For a brief moment you can be in control of your mind, rather than the other way round.

That is the ability that gives the car you are driving a super-charging effect. You are not now limited to automatically responding to whatever sensory stimulus that comes along.

Most of the time your mind is a stimulus/response machine: The senses get stimulated by something, and the mind automatically responds. Through this you can demonstrate the power you have to break that automaticity. That you can stop the mind automatically responding and can consciously control yourself to observe the mind, and then make a considered response to what is going on.

That is like harnessing the power of the atom, rather than merely moving atoms around to make things.

Chapter 3

Spirituality

Aged 25 – "I can tell you what's going on –
But that might not tell you what is going on"

I had never really been interested in "spirituality".
It seemed somehow fey, in the excessively refined sense of the word. Not something that could deal with the slings and arrows that I felt coming my way in real life.
That changed on the trip to the Himalayas. I suddenly got the sense that there might be a way "through": That the other world-liness which I had glimpsed on the side of the mountain might be able to take me out of my daily pain management.
Maybe sex and drugs and rock and roll weren't the long-term solution.
I came back from India with an idea that there might be some value in it; hence my still wearing Indian clothes and going vegetarian.
I had one lead. A friend of mine had "got religion" of the Indian kind and sold all his possessions to visit his guru in India. I had benefited to the tune of two huge Ditton 15 speakers that I picked up for a song from him.
He was back now and I went to visit him in his farmhouse near Bristol.
"Right, yeah," he said. "What do you want to know?"
"Well, er, what is it all about? Where do you start?"
"You are in everything, and everything is in you."
"What?"
"You are in everything, and everything is in you."
This was going to be hard.

I explained that this was not much help and he shrugged his shoulders enigmatically and said,

"Well, you could always read Paramhansa Yogananda's 'Autobiography of a Yogi'.

He had a copy to hand and I removed myself from his presence and went home to be enlightened.

I devoured it – page by page, word by word.

It didn't tell me much about me, but it told me all about him. And the thing that came across is that he "knew". Shot through as it was with quirky tales of gurus, non-eating saints, and all sorts of jiggery-pokery, what rang true was that there was another dimension to life that was accessible. He had experienced it; I wanted to experience it too.

At the back of the book was an address in California that would send you lessons in something called Kriya Yoga. Send $25 and they would send you the lessons by sea mail.

I sent them $50 and told them to send it by air.

Within days I was sat on an upright chair in my bedroom focussing on "a place between your eyes" and breathing deeply. Nothing much happened. It might be because, although I had temporarily given up tobacco as a nod to my new spiritual quest, I was still out every evening in clubs or at parties, so my meditation had to be in the morning after I got up and before I went to work, which would be about 10.30am.

I soon got bored. However, I was still very much on the spiritual trail.

I read everything I could get hold of. I did courses and self-awareness seminars. I meditated before going to work, and I tried to pick up the more spiritual girls that I came across.

After a while I had come to the conclusion that there was such a thing as enlightenment, and I wanted it.

Amazingly, I had the experience that I was looking for.

I had been on the spiritual search for all of 7 months, and it happened.

Before I tell you what actually did happen, I want to say that I know it will sound trite. But there really is no way to adequately express the inexpressible.

Whatever you say will sound unremarkable.

"Well... I was sitting under this tree... I think it was a banyan when suddenly...."

You try it.

I also want to say that I do not think that the experience that I had was "the" experience, in the sense that it is the experience that everyone has to have to "get enlightened".

It was just the experience I had that moved me on from thinking of myself as an individual living my own separate life, to realising that I was a part of something bigger.

Finally, one more codicil to the description I am about to give you.

There is a famous scene in the film Solaris *(George Clooney's version) where George's character asks one of the engineers on the space station, "What's going on here?"*

The engineer replies, "I can tell you what's going on; but that might not tell you what is going on." The same applies here.

I am going to tell you the experience that I had, but it still might mean absolutely nothing to you.

I was sitting in a room with a group of friends one evening. Not my house, someone else's. We were listening to some music, Lowell George I think.

Someone asked me if I played the guitar. I did not.

"Well," they said, "why not try listening to the music and see if you can play along with it."

When I reflected on it afterwards the conclusion I came to was that, somehow, I had focused on this music in such a way that it shut out all my other senses, and as a result I was able to get beyond my mind's insistence as to what was real and what was not real, and so this new dimension was able to open up to me. What actually happened was that my perception of the nature of reality shifted dramatically.

Whereas normally I look out and I see people, in a space that is contained by the periphery of my vision, suddenly I felt myself to be a part of something infinitely greater than myself. It was as if I was a glove puppet, and there was something hugely vast that was both containing me and everything around me.

And I suddenly understood what it meant to "see the light".

Not some ethereal understanding, but actual light.

This "light" was coming from somewhere behind me, in my consciousness, and it manifested in tiny optical fibres that came through me. I was seeing those fibres as they came through my eyes and connected with everything I saw in front of me, in the room.

Everything was made of light. That light came through my consciousness, created all that I saw in front of me, and then seemed to disappear into infinity.

I was a part of something much bigger than myself. Whatever it was, it was creating me and allowing me to see my connection, through those optical fibres, with everything else in the room.

Two things struck me.

First that all things were interconnected; not just in the sense that all things relate together, but also in that this light seemed to be a vehicle through which all this was manifesting.

Secondly that there was a "greater being"; something was holding this together. There was a fundamental order to life. I was a part of that order, and so was everything I was looking at. In an instant I recognised the experience as exactly fitting the descriptions of enlightenment that I had read about. I understood what my friend had meant when he said, "You are in everything, and everything is in you."

Suddenly everything went "clunk-click", and I knew that this was what I had been wanting to experience.

No one else in the room saw anything. I said, "WOW" a few times, and tried to explain what I was seeing, but it did not hold much interest.

All in all the experience lasted about three hours.

I went home and just sat and stared into space.

I did not emerge from my flat for three days, but when I did I saw everything in a different light. It was as if I had seen "Outside" for the first time.

It was true. It existed.

I was amazed that people seemed to be going about their lives, not knowing the full nature of the reality of the life that they were living.

Newsreaders made no reference to this interconnectedness. In fact everyone lived their lives as if they were completely separate from each other, as I had done only a few days before.

I was faced with a dilemma: What was I to do about it?

It was as if I had been invited to a drinks party at 10 Downing Street.

Halfway through the evening I needed to pee, so went to the loo. I opened the door, and there sitting on the loo was the Prime Minister. Not only was he sitting on the loo, but his head was resting somewhere by his feet, and where his head should have been, there was the head of an alien monster.

*Stunned, I closed the door; the Prime Minister was an alien. What's more **I knew** that the Prime minister was an alien.*

I was faced with a choice. Did I go out into the party and say, "Hey, guys, guess what, the Prime Minister is an alien," and have everyone think I was completely bonkers; or did I carry on with my life and just pretend that it had not happened?

That was my dilemma now.

Did I tell everyone what I had seen ("Lock him up quick before he does any damage to himself, or to us"), or did I think of it as an aberration and try to forget it.

I did try to forget it. I forced myself to go out and see everything

as being separate, but I never got further than the end of the road. It just fitted so perfectly. It just made sense. And so gradually I accepted it. I came to the conclusion that, for whatever reason, I had been given a glimpse into something. Not only that, but I was in a place where that understanding of the nature of reality was not common knowledge.
I almost felt that it was my duty to communicate what I had seen.

I was working in advertising at the time, so a few days later I walked into Saatchi and Saatchi and resigned.
They thought I was mad. I probably was.
Tim Bell asked to see me.
"It has taken you three years to get this job. We have just won the General Election and Mrs Thatcher is in power, do you really want to throw it all away for some whim? You'll regret it."

In the end I did walk, and to this day I have never regretted it.
I have never had the same experience again, but every day I see echoes of it in the way that life works.
In the beauty that is all around me.
In the way that human beings treat each other.
In the violence that comes from not understanding our true nature, and what we mean to each other.
And in the way that life works itself out in each of us.
There is a famous story reported about Albert Einstein:[5]
When asked by a reporter something like, "What, in your opinion, is the most important question facing humanity today?" Albert Einstein thought for a bit then replied, "I think the most important question facing humanity is, 'Is the universe a friendly place?' This is the first and most basic question all people must answer for themselves.
"For if we decide that the universe is an unfriendly place, then we will use our technology, our scientific discoveries and our

natural resources to achieve safety and power by creating bigger walls to keep out the unfriendliness and bigger weapons to destroy all that which is unfriendly and I believe that we are getting to a place where technology is powerful enough that we may either completely isolate or destroy ourselves as well in this process.

"If we decide that the universe is neither friendly nor unfriendly and that God is essentially 'playing dice with the universe', then we are simply victims to the random toss of the dice and our lives have no real purpose or meaning.

"But if we decide that the universe is a friendly place, then we will use our technology, our scientific discoveries and our natural resources to create tools and models for understanding that universe. Because power and safety will come through understanding its workings and its motives."

I had discovered that the universe was a friendly place.

A bridge to a new understanding

Understanding.

That is one of the purposes of developing consciousness; and through understanding comes the ability to live one's life more skilfully.

As we develop an understanding of how life works and what motivates us, how the world works and how it all fits together, so we start to glimpse the basic premise upon which all life is built, and so we can build our lives, taking that premise into consideration.

Is the universe a friendly place or not? The key question according to Einstein. And it is. It changes everything. If the universe is a friendly place, and a good definition of the word friend, is "someone you can trust", then it affects the whole way that you look at life.

It means that your starting point is not that there is you, and there is everything else, and that you have to survive at all costs – the basic programme of the mind.

Instead there is a fundamental force that conspires to support and develop all life. That in some way we are upheld, and, through some strange mechanism, are encouraged to grow and develop through the events that occur in our lives.

At this point one would normally veer into arguments about God.

Does God exist? If he does why do babies starve? What about the Holocaust? What proof is there of God? And before long we are in Richard Dawkins-land, or Religion-land, depending on your point of view.

I want to suspend those judgements for the moment, and remind us that this book is about developing consciousness, not comparing theories or beliefs.

What we are about is looking into our own consciousness and asking, "What is true for me?" Not in the sense that all truth is subjective and therefore whatever is true for me is ultimately the truth. But in the sense of "con-scios" – knowing together. What is true for me, and can I compare that truth to the truth that others experience, and therefore draw some conclusions about what is ultimately true for all of us?

If I see wood nymphs at the bottom of my garden, that might be true for me. But if I can find no other evidence that others also see those wood nymphs, I might have to start to consider the possibility that these nymphs might be a hallucination.

In the same way, if we are looking at our experience, it does not help us to merely consider what we believe and what others believe, agreeing with some and disagreeing with others. Doing this is just second-hand research – we are letting others do the thinking for us and then seeing what we can agree with. That is different from looking at our experience and asking if others experience the same thing.

So we will not veer into the God territory, and all the beliefs that are involved with it. Instead we will ask ourselves, "What have *I* experienced?" What can I say is true for me?

Over the last section of the book I have simply written down what has been true for me. What has shaped me, what has happened, and how I have reacted. In the end I have come to the conclusion that the universe is a friendly place. That there is some kind of interconnectedness that holds the whole thing together and which fundamentally supports us.

I spoke earlier of the idea that we are not our minds. That we are able to step outside our minds and begin to see the nature of the mind.

The Dalai Lama suggested that this nature of the mind is nothing material, and therefore can not be measured in a material way, only experienced as the fundamental nature of our consciousness.

If we assume this to be the case – and the fact that we have some control over our minds, as well as the ability to observe them, suggests that this might be so – then we can start to look at the universe being a friendly place from the standpoint of how the nature of our minds connects with the nature of everything else.

I experienced a fundamental interconnectedness that seemed to be linked with, and yet was greater than, my consciousness. It was as if my mind was the software, and what I now experienced was that this software was running on some greater operating system. Something that I had previously been unaware of.

I experienced that connection through something I saw, and it created a bridge to a new understanding of the way that the world was working.

Such a bridge might become evident through any one of the senses. Through hearing (some call that "the music of the spheres") which has this interconnectedness as a harmonic, a geometrical and mystical pattern that is appreciated through hearing.

Some might experience it through touch or feeling; some through taste or smell.

In fact there are as many ways of experiencing this interconnectedness as there are ways into our consciousness. Because if it is true, if there is a fundamental interconnectedness in life, and if we can experience it, then all roads lead to that truth. However we travel there, we will all end up at the same destination, if we are really looking at developing our consciousness.

The pursuit of this truth is what is known as spirituality.

We are not really interested in theories

Rowan Williams describes spirituality as, "The cultivation of a sensitive and rewarding relationship with eternal truth and love."[6]

It is an amazing definition, because it perfectly captures the nature of spirituality without falling into any religious traps.

He talks of it being *cultivation* which suggests action. It requires our attention, like growing something. We have to tend it; work out what conditions will enable it to grow best. What nourishment it requires. It takes time and is a process.

He talks about *sensitivity*. Spirituality is never abusive; it requires us to feel our way through it – to sense, appraise and readjust.

It is *rewarding* in that it enriches us.

And it is a *relationship* – we are therefore required to relate, through our sensitivity, to this "other", that we are in fact a part of.

And he describes this *other* as eternal truth and love.

Again, I do not propose to go into a huge amount of detail as to what this means, but if you simply split the words up, it speaks of the eternal, which has a timeless quality about it; it speaks of truth, which is the actual nature of reality, and it speaks of love, which I will define as "self-giving".

All of which you can sign me up for.

Spirituality is obviously about our spirit, and the definition of "spirit" is the essence of who we are. It is the distillation of our very core.

So spirituality is the cultivation of that essence, and the way it might possibly link into something that is greater than itself.

Hence a spiritual experience tends to be one where the essence of who we are seems to be given meaning by a greater whole, as in the experience I described a few pages back..

It is not something unreal. On the contrary, it involves us becoming aware of who we really are, what our essence actually is, and then seeing how that essence connects with the essence of all other things in the universe.

And, once again, we are not really interested in theories. We are interested in what we have experienced in our own consciousness. What does that tell us about the essence of who we are and how that connects us to all other things?

You might say that you do not believe in "the eternal", that concepts of spirituality hold no meaning for you as they have not been proven by science, and therefore you cannot see how this could possibly relate to you.

But think about it. When you say that you want it to be proven, what you really mean is that you want it to fit in with the concepts of science that great minds have developed over the years. That your mind wants to satisfy itself that its understanding of how the world works, which it has developed in conjunction with other minds, fits with provable criteria that can be demonstrated over and over again in experiments.

If you consider yourself to be your mind, then that is probably an end of the matter

But, if you are not your mind, if you have the facility to

observe your mind, if you have the capability to self-reflect and develop some aspect of self-awareness, then it is possible for you to come to an understanding, through your consciousness, of the essence of who you are and how that essence relates to the rest of the universe.

We have already heard that the Dalai Lama speaks of our consciousness, the very essence of who we are (therefore our spirit), as having no material form.

That it cannot be measured by scientific means. It can only be experienced for what it is – that essence.

So I ask you to consider that in yourself as we proceed.

How much of this has been, or could be, true for you?

What is your actual experience of the nature of your life, as opposed to what others have told you it is, or what you have come to believe?

When we begin to look at that, we begin to go beyond the constraints that are put upon us by our minds, and the minds of others.

When we begin to allow that pattern to move, and not have the mind press it back into focus.

When we will allow our mind not to be made up as to what is "out there", or "in here"; but instead allow it to look and see what it sees, as it is seeing it – then we can make progress.

Then we can develop our consciousness consciously, rather than allow it to be formed by a series of assumptions made by ours, and other minds.

Which is to say nothing more than to be open.

Open to the possibility that you might not know: That even your dearest beliefs may not be true (they *may* be true, but also hold the possibility that they may not be true).

Open to what you might experience through your consciousness.

Open to what you might already have experienced through your consciousness, but have since discounted.

Open to looking at your life and what really motivates you.

Open to being moved.

Open to being surprised.

Open to finding out who you really are, and how you relate to all that is around you.

Divine Consciousness

So, as in the film *Solaris*, I am now going to tell you what *I* think is going on.

This is the part of the book where I lay my cards on the table and say this is it. This is that simple explanation of what enlightenment is.

This is what people say that you have to be prepared for before you can be told.

This is the pearl that must not be cast before swine.

This is what is whispered in your ear when you are ready to hear it.

Supposedly.

I offer it to you not as gospel, but just by way of an idea that explains it for me. The whole of the book leads up to this chapter. The rest of the book, and the rest of our lives are spent unpacking what this might mean to us.

It is a statement of fact to say that we are the only ones who experience our lives. All you have ever experienced has come to you, and only you. You are completely alone.

No matter how close other people come to you, they can never experience what you experience. They might communicate to you that they are experiencing similar things, but it is all hearsay. You are the only one who experiences your life.

For most of the time you do that through your consciousness.

As we have discussed, your senses tell you what is going on, and your mind works out a picture of the nature of reality.

Then there is your unconscious.

Your unconscious is all the things that you are experiencing, however, you are not consciously doing so: Your dreams; how your heart beats; you are not conscious of healing yourself, but your body does it all the same; growing; aging; bodily functions – many of them go on unconsciously.

Carl Jung put forward the idea that we all have very deep memories – passed on from our families, from the race we are a part of, and from things that we have forgotten that we were previously conscious of. He suggested that these govern the way we behave as we unconsciously make decisions about our lives based on our past.

For example, if we were denied love at an early age we might make a decision that intimate relationships between people were not available to us, and we might therefore have a great deal of difficulty forming normal family relationships in our later life.

Jung's idea was that the part of our mind that we are conscious of is only the tip of a huge iceberg, and that if we are not careful the decisions made and left in the unconscious area will come to rule us, like the tail wagging the dog.

Psychologists also suggest that we can see what sort of decisions we have made in the past by the behaviour we can observe ourselves doing in the present.

That is the basis for the therapy and analysis that many people now undergo: Looking into their past, trying to identify unconscious decisions that make us behave in a certain way; and then trying to "unmake" those decisions to free our behaviour.

All this takes place within our unconscious.

So we have that which we are conscious of, and that which we are unconscious of.

I want to suggest that there is another level of consciousness, and this is the level that people become aware of when they become enlightened, and this I have called "Divine

Consciousness".

Divine because it relates to "supreme being". If there is inter-connectedness, and if the universe is a friendly place, and if we are a part of some consciousness that is greater than ourselves, it is supreme. You could equally call it Cosmic Consciousness, as the origins of the word "cosmos" suggest an ordering principle. However, I have gone for Divine Consciousness as it sits easier with me. Divine or Cosmic, it does not matter, because in this context the key word is Consciousness.

What is important is that the whole issue of enlightenment comes down to a reality that exists within us. That as we develop our consciousness and become aware of what is within us, we begin to be able to see that we too are a part of that which is within us. In fact it is the essence of who we are.

This Divine Consciousness is common to all sentient beings. It is the spiritual DNA that makes up all life.

All plants and animals, rocks, books, clothes, carpets, curtains, in fact everything that *is* comes from this spiritual DNA. And the unique thing we have as human beings is that we can experience it, and reflect on that experience.

Other animals might experience it, we cannot say. But we can experience it, and be aware of what we are experiencing.

When someone becomes what we call "enlightened", what it really means is that they have experienced this basic aspect of their consciousness. That, for whatever reason, their minds have suspended their insistence that there is a "me", and there is an "out there", and have come to the experience of the interconnect-edness of all things – Divine Consciousness.

And more than that. This Divine Consciousness is common to all of us. If we all plumbed back into our consciousness, through our unconscious, we would all hit the bedrock of this Divine Consciousness.

We all share a commonwealth, and that commonwealth is the Divine Consciousness that gives us everything

All of us share an understanding of consciousness. That is where we generally live our lives. That is the area that science investigates, that the news talks about. The bit we chat about with others. That is where televisions are bought and sold, and where we make our breakfast and feed ourselves.

Next comes our unconscious. This aspect of life lives in our minds and our bodies. Much of it drives us in an automatic way, however, occasionally we become conscious of it and might share it with others. Science tries to measure it, but most of it does not lend itself to this measurement.

Then there is Divine Consciousness that is common to all of us.

If you were to burrow deeply back into my consciousness you would hit that Divine Consciousness. If you were to burrow deeply back into your consciousness, you would hit Divine Consciousness. It is actually a shared consciousness, and from it comes our interconnectedness.

Our true brotherhood and sisterhood as human beings does not just come from the fact that we are all descended from the same origin, or from the fact that we are all animals. It comes from that shared consciousness.

When one person is enlightened he or she will experience that interconnectedness. When two people become enlightened together they will experience that shared consciousness from which the interconnectedness comes.

And the implications of this are endless.

If we are all from the same consciousness, and if we are all simply different manifestations of the same supreme being, then war is meaningless.

War comes from fear. The fear that others will overtake us leads to the need to defend ourselves against that threat, as

Einstein was arguing.

If we are all cut from the same block, then there is fundamentally nothing to be afraid of, and all fear is based upon the illusion of separation.

That is not to say that we should not fear the madman that is coming towards us with a knife. Just that the reason that the madman is coming towards us, because you have something he wants or whatever it might be, is based upon an illusion.

If we all come from the same consciousness, if we are all fundamentally different aspects of the same supreme being, and if we all share the infinite resources that this supreme being has to offer, then there is enough of everything for everybody.

The idea that we have to protect our resources, that there should be people with vast amounts of wealth in the world, and others with nothing, is just brought about by the illusion that there is not enough to go round, and that therefore we all have to fight for what we can get.

It is as if there were 1000 pieces of chocolate in a bowl, and 100 children. There is enough to go round; but because of the fear of not getting any all the children fight for the chocolate, leaving some with 50 pieces, and some with none. That is the history of the world.

I am not saying that we all should give everything away and start again. What I am saying is that fundamentally we all share a commonwealth, and that commonwealth is the divine consciousness that gives us everything.

It gives us our current consciousness. It gives us the capacity to have that consciousness. It gave us our lives; it brought us into being. And the purpose it gave us in our lives was to become conscious of itself.

"Realisation" Number One: You are always in exactly the right place to be able to take the next step.

Realisation Number Two: You are not your mind.

Realization Number Three: The entire purpose and meaning of your life is to awaken you to this level of consciousness.
Everything that has happened to you in your life points you towards uncovering this truth for yourself. Every desire you have ever had is founded upon the desire to realize that "you are in everything, and everything is in you".

Deep inside yourself, if you are able to reach it, is a consciousness that you can awaken to. For most of our lives we are unconscious of this, and think that we are separate from everything; but this is like being asleep.

Everything in our life points towards this – the primacy of love, the need to excel and create, the need to amass wealth. All of it is motivated by this fundamental consciousness demanding to be experienced. We might misunderstand the cry within us, and instead interpret it as being a need that we have to control others, but behind it all is the simple realisation of the truth of our interconnectedness.

If you follow this line, then evolution is not just about the physical evolution of the body to survive and become more successful. The next step of evolution will not be the elongation of our two thumbs for better texting.

Evolution is about the evolution of consciousness.

As consciousness developed from plants to animals to humans, in whatever order and over whatever time, that development has been a function of its increasing awareness of the extent of itself, and of its capacity to develop.

The next stage of evolution could be the development of the awareness of this divine consciousness that is common to us all. It is continually demanding that we become conscious of it, and we are continually resisting it.

You do not have to be enlightened to be enlightened

You do not have to be enlightened to be enlightened.

By this I mean that I am not suggesting that it is necessary to have some "peak experience" in order to become awakened to the interconnectedness of all life.

What we are looking at, in developing our consciousness, is an understanding of the nature of the reality that we live in. This enables us to live our lives more skilfully.

You do not actually experience gravity. Yes we know that you do not float off into the air, but the reason you think of it as gravity is because that is what you have been told. Galileo showed that the earth was round, Newton saw the apple drop, and consequently we have an explanation of the nature of our reality called gravity.

Even before people understood the laws of gravity they knew to make a table with four legs, that houses needed foundations, and that if you dropped a rock from a great height it would kill someone. All this was firmly understood by everyone without knowing the whys and the wherefores.

Similarly it is not necessary to have had a direct experience of divine consciousness for you to accept the principle that this level of consciousness does exist and that it is worth basing your life upon the principles that such an interconnectedness suggests.

Take the example of those 3D Magic Eye pictures.

Some people can see them, some can't. It does not matter. The fact is that the image is there, whether you can see it or not.

In any random roomful of people about half are able to see a "Magic Eye" effect. The other half are not able to see it. The important question is can you accept that there is another image there, even if you cannot see it?

If you *can* see it, there is no problem and you can use the picture knowing that there is a 3D image hidden within it.

If you cannot see the image, then you have to decide whether or not you can assume that it is there, based on what others say.

The same is true about experiencing divine consciousness.

You may or may not have already had an experience that chimes completely with what I am saying.

If you have had such an experience, then developing consciousness is about exploring the possibilities and ramifications of that experience.

If you cannot say that you have had such an experience, then it becomes about exploring whether or not the existence of such a level of consciousness might have an effect on your life, and how one can discover the principles behind the nature of that reality, so as to build one's life upon it.

There is also a middle way.

That is to recognise experiences that you have had in your life as pointing to the existence of that level of consciousness, while not having had a complete realisation of that experience.

Instead you have had glimpses – maybe moments alone in nature, or with someone special, or while reading a book, or during key events; all of which point towards a greater reality.

That is the place that most of us exist at, and it enables us to foster an understanding of the possibilities that are open to us when we live our lives assuming that there is something greater than ourselves.

The important thing is not the experience itself. That experience is impossible to manufacture, it just comes. Some people have it, and some people don't. And the people that have it are no better than the people who do not have it. In fact in some cases, if one is not fully prepared for the experience, it can lead to a situation where our mind *identifies* with the experience as being something it *possesses*, and therefore can lead to a deluded form of egotistical insanity (I am *the one* etc...).

It is worth taking the time to consider whether or not you *can* live with the idea that there is a level of consciousness that gives us a glimpse into the fundamental building blocks of life, and that shows all things to be interconnected. To admit to that changes one's whole outlook on life.

It admits to the possibility of order, where previously there was just chaos.

It enables a real experience of kinship for all human beings. In fact for all plants and animals, and for the planet itself.

It opens us up to limitless possibilities in terms of the intelligence that is available to us, and consequently the resources that we can draw upon in forming relationships that work for the good of the whole.

And it shows us how we can experience a peace and contentment in life, rather than continue with the struggle to overcome "Contra Mundum" (against the world).

Like a fish trying to describe a cash register

It is definitely worth reflecting on your own life experience to see how this fits in with the way that you have developed your view of life. It seems to me to be all about feeling separate and feeling connected. Maybe think of times when you have really felt connected: when something or someone seemed to almost be a part of you. When it seemed that the work you were doing almost became who you were. Or when you felt an unexplainable link with nature, or a certain place. It might be that you had a feeling of being a part of something greater than yourself, either within or outside a religious context. Maybe you have had experiences with your family, or with close friends. Maybe related to some specific activity, or just a state of mind.

Take time to think about it.

The way that we build up our world-view in life is all about con-scios; knowing together. Listening to the experience of others, and how they have viewed their lives, and then comparing that to our own experience. You can then connect up the dots and see what a picture it makes for you.

Developing consciousness is about continually reflecting on that picture to see what common themes exist and what conclusions we can draw about the nature of reality, and the laws and principles that govern that reality.

Could we come to a conclusion, as Einstein suggested, that the universe is a friendly place; that there is a fundamental connectedness between all things that we are a part of?

If so, then nothing is ever the same again.

You then have something completely reliable as you work out, day by day, how to live your life.

It is a key piece of information that changes the picture of the way the world works. It means that everything that you do will have a direct effect on others around you. That in some deep way, it is not just about what you say and do, but the very nature of how you interact with the universe around you. Your connection is on such a deep level, that it can never be undone; it is the very essence of life that brought you into being, and also brought everyone else into being.

Your connection to that "ground of being" is through your consciousness. It brought you into life, it gave you the facility to be conscious, and it gave you all the things that you could be conscious of – your world. But more than that, it gave you the ability to be conscious of *it*, and it built into your software the desire for co-consciousness. A desire to know the interconnectedness of all things, and that which brings about that interconnectedness.

All through mineral, plant, animal and human history there has been a continual pull towards that consciousness, so that now, in our time, in only the last few thousand years, we have begun to be aware of this deeper level.

Now is the time for the awareness of the now that has always been.

In the past we have not understood it. We have made

religions out of it, we have believed it to be our minds, we have argued about its existence; but still it calls us to become conscious of it. It calls us to know the deeper nature of life.

Our response depends on the level of our understanding.

It can be translated into the simple will to live, into the desire to create, the desire for riches and fame, the desire to love and to care, and finally the desire to fully know that nature for what it is; the ground of all being.

We are obviously entering "God" territory now.

But God is just the word we have come up with to describe this deeper nature. Even people who believe in God cannot say who or what God is. It is just a word that we use for our convenience to describe that which is supreme in our lives. It is a human construct; a reaction to the sense of the existence of something more than ourselves.

It is the pet name we have created for that beingness – like daddy or mummy.

It attempts to frame a relationship that is unframeable.

Through it we give the supreme being attributes that we have come to recognise through our humanity. We can understand humanity, and so we use it when we come to describe God.

But in reality, for us to try to describe that supreme being is like a fish trying to describe a cash register.

There are about 5 leaps in reality to get to it: From water based living, to air based living; to the need for barter, for a value to be placed on things, for money to be invented, and for a machine to be invented to count money.

An inconceivable leap.

So it is when we try to understand God.

Chapter 4

The Tradition of Mystical Reality

Just realise where you come from: This is the essence of wisdom

What I am talking about is not a new idea.

In his book *The Perennial Philosophy*,[7] Aldous Huxley defines Leibniz's phrase "Philosophia perennis" as:

> "The metaphysic that recognises a Divine Reality substantial to the word of things and lives and minds;
>
> The psychology that finds in the soul something similar to, or even identical with, Divine Reality;
>
> The ethic that places man's final ending the knowledge of the immanent and transcendent ground of all being – the thing is immemorial and universal."

He goes on to say that:

> "Rudiments of the Perennial Philosophy may be found among the traditionary lore of primitive peoples in every region of the world, and in its fully developed forms it has a place in every one of the higher religions.
>
> A version of this Highest Common Factor in all preceding and subsequent theologies was first committed to writing more than twenty-five centuries ago, and since that time the inexhaustible theme has been treated again and again, from the standpoint of every religious tradition and in all the principle languages of Asia and Europe."

And so it is.

Everywhere you look this same experience of consciousness is treated in different ways.

The mystic Bede Griffiths says:[8]

"The goal of each religion is the same.

It is the absolute, transcendent state, the one Reality, the eternal Truth, which cannot be expressed, cannot be conceived.

This is the goal not only of all religion, but of all human existence — whether they like it or not, all men are continually attracted by this transcendent Truth.

The intellect, in and beyond every formulation by which it seeks to express its thought, is in search of the Absolute.

It is made for Being itself, for Truth, for Reality, and it cannot rest satisfied in any partial truth, in any construction of the human mind. It is always being carried beyond itself to the ultimate Truth."

Similar writing over the ages shows that there was an awareness of the experience, and that it was expressed in different ways in different cultures.

The Tao Te Ching is a traditional Chinese text written about the 6th century BC by Lao-tzu. It is a wonderful book of wisdom divided into 81 short poems. They are very readable, at least in the translation by Stephen Mitchell that I own. Perfect for reading one a day.

Lao-tzu actually just means "old man". Nothing much is known about him, however, the legend is that he was a venerable old monk. When he retired he was travelling to a distant mountain cave where he was to spend the rest of his life meditating. He came to a river where a boatman ran a ferry. He asked the boatman to take him across.

"What will you give me as payment?" asked the boatman.

"I have nothing," said Lao-tzu, "except my wisdom."

"Write down what you know," said the boatman,
and so the Tao Te Ching came into existence.
It covers the same subject we are covering now.
Stephen Mitchell's translation of stanza 14 says:[9]

Look and it can't be seen.
Listen and it can't be heard.
Reach and it can't be grasped.

Above, it isn't bright.
Below it isn't dark.
Seamless, unnameable,
it returns to the realm of nothing.
form that includes all forms,
image without an image,
subtle, beyond all conception.

Approach it and there is no beginning;
follow it and there is no end.
You can't know it, but you can be it,
At ease in your own life.
Just realise where you come from:
This is the essence of wisdom.

Again it is the same theme approached from a different
perspective.

The idea of something that is unknowable, but which you
can be – *form that includes all forms – just realise where you come*
from.

And again, right up to modern times, Rowan Williams writes in
his book *Ponder These Things:*[10]

"The church is, as Eastern theology has consistently said, the

'divine humanity' of Christ, human nature restored and trans-
figured by the presence of divine 'energy' saturating yet not
destroying it."

A very similar picture of the nature of reality.

Again and again, in almost every tradition we come back to the
same subject, a divine reality upon which all things are based,
and which is accessible to us.

In his book *The Power of Now,* Eckhart Tollë says:[11]

"Zen masters use the word satori to describe a flash of insight, a
moment of no-mind and total presence. Although satori is not
lasting, be grateful when it comes, for it gives you a taste of enlightenment. You may, indeed, have experienced it many times without
knowing what it is or realising its importance... Beyond the beauty
of external forms, there is more here: something that cannot be
named, something ineffable, some deep, inner, holy essence.
Whenever and wherever there is beauty, this inner essence shines
through somehow. It only reveals itself to you when you are present.
Could it be that this nameless essence and your presence are one and
the same? Would it be there without your presence? Go deeply into
it. Find out for yourself."

Aged 35 – "I'm looking for Mohammed"

A bicentennial does not happen very often.
The French were celebrating theirs with a huge parade and
spectacle at the Place de la Concorde; the exact spot where the
guillotine did most of its business during the reign of terror.
For weeks, as I drove in to work, I saw them constructing the
huge stage where Jessye Norman was to perform in front of the

crowds. Then they cast stands all around the place. There was to be a parade of all nations, followed by the concert and a spectacular firework display.

The day before the event I decided to walk down to try and get tickets.

"Mais non," said the gendarme on duty on the Champs-Elysées. "Those seats are for 'Les Privilèges', you will have to stand and watch from here."

I wandered down the Champs towards the newly erected stands opposite the Hotel Crillon. There didn't seem to be much security, so I walked up to the entrance to one of the stands that rose about 30 feet high in front of me, completely obscuring everything the other side. There were stairs leading up the side which I began to climb.

As I reached the top I saw the whole of the Place de La Concorde in front of me, magnificently dressed with a huge stage, flags, lights and a massive sound system.

I stood and stared. After a few moments one of the workmen came over to me.

"Bonjour," I said, and we fell into conversation about his work putting it all together.

"I like your sunglasses," he said.

I handed them to him. "Have them."

He took off the pair he was wearing and we swapped.

"Any chance of getting tickets for tomorrow?"

"Sure," he said, "just come along and ask for me, my name is Mohammed."

I thanked him and left the way I had come.

The next day I planned to arrive early.

The event started at 5.00pm, so I arrived at noon, only to find the Champs-Elysées lined with people 10 deep from the Arc de Triomphe, down to Concorde.

As I walked the route I found that the only gaps were for streets, and for the entrance to the Crillon Hotel.

At the Crillon world leaders were coming and going. In front of the Hotel the stands were ringed with police. One ring around the stands with policeman facing out – a policeman every 10 yards – and another ring all the way round the pavements, again one every 10 yards facing the street with crash barriers behind them. There was no way through those barriers, except by the exit from the Crillon. I decided to try.

As the gate opened a car came out and I moved forward. Inside the car was Rajiv Gandhi. I lost my nerve.

A few minutes later another car came and I walked forward past the barrier and into the street lined on both sides with policemen. It was only 15 yards across the road, but took ages. I walked slowly and with intent into the open space of the road, policemen everywhere I looked, me on my own.

As I got to the stand on the other side of the road I fixed an official in the eye and said "I'm looking for Mohammed, he works up there," and I pointed to where I had been the day before.

I was not challenged and managed to make my way to the top of the stairs.

Again the whole of the Place de La Concorde lay before me, with two huge circular stands fanning out left and right from the Champs-Elysées. There was no sign of Mohammed; I was the only person on any of the stands – it was deserted.

What to do next? There were four hours till the parade started. I decided to wait.

After an hour cleaners came and swept the area.

Then the police came with their dogs.

I stood completely motionless and looked back along the side of the stand, up the Champs-Elysées, towards l'Etoile.

I stood and stared.

It was as if I was not there. The police came up to me with their dogs and walked around me. No one said a word.

Next came the usherettes with blue sashes looking like stewardesses. The stands were made up of rows of benches, and on each place they put a programme and a tiny spyglass.

Finally came "Les Privilèges". Finely dressed in sub-evening wear they filled up the benches, which were not numbered. I was wearing a shirt and tie, so fitted in.

Before long the stands were full, and I was safe.

I got chatting to the woman next to me who was a journalist for the Irish Times. She said that this stand was for Embassy staff and their guests.

I think the person on my right was the Foreign Minister of Uruguay.

We exchanged pleasantries and I said I was from Great Britain. Before too long we were best friends, both excited about the parade ahead. There were thousands of people all around us.

It began with marching bands; one from each country. As each band came past the Embassy representatives stood in turn to take the salute. My Uruguayan friend was soon on his feet with a grand salute.

Towards the rear was the British band, from one of the Guards Regiments. As it wove into sight the foreign minister grabbed me and motioned for me to stand. I resisted for a moment, but seeing that he thought it was the done thing, I got to my feet and took the salute as the band leader threw his head to the right and faced me. No one else moved. The band marched past, eyes right. Eventually I sat down, feeling a little drained, and let the rest of the show wash over me.

At the end we all got up from our seats and were ushered down the staircase.

The police had laid a channel of crash barriers through the crowd right up to the tube station at Madeleine. It was a rat run to get Les Privilèges out and away from the half a million people that broke through into the street at the end of the show.

As we passed through the channel it was magically removed by the policemen standing beside it, so we were left, safe from the mayhem, on the dry land of the Madeleine pavement.

Christianity should be considered as an 'Eastern religion'

This radical understanding of the nature of reality is even present in the Christian religion.

It is the last place that many would look for enlightenment. But when you read the words of Jesus closely, there it is.

Most of the time when Jesus is asked about something he goes off on a long description about birds of the air and fish of the sea or corn and stony ground. However, there are times when he is asked a direct question about the nature of reality.

At one point he is asked, "Where is the kingdom of heaven?" In other words where is God? Because the best definition of 'heaven' is really 'where God is'. Nowadays we often see heaven as the place that you go to when you die, but that is not the answer that Jesus gives.

He says in Luke's Gospel, "The kingdom of Heaven does not come with your careful observation, nor will people say, 'Here it is,' or 'There it is,' because the Kingdom of Heaven is within you."[12]

That is an amazing piece of information. He does not point to the sky, go into parables, or beat about the bush in any way. He says that the Kingdom of Heaven is within you.

Within you.

To my mind this chimes with exactly what we are talking about. The concept of an inner reality with a supreme being that is available to us through our consciousness.

And he goes further.

In the Gospel of John he says, "On that day you will realize that I am in my Father, and you are in me, and I am in you."[12]

Again, this is pretty similar to "you are in everything and everything is in you".

If you look at how Jesus is explaining it here, he is saying that, "I (Jesus) exist in that divine consciousness. You exist within my reality, framed by that divine consciousness; and I exist in your reality, that is also framed by that divine consciousness."

In other words he is stating that we share a common experience in that divine consciousness. We all exist within the reality that it creates for us.

And this conceptualisation of the nature of reality is not limited to the four Gospels.

In the letter to the Corinthians Paul speaks of, "God's secret wisdom, a wisdom that has been hidden and that God destined for our glory before time began."[12]

It is the truth that Jesus says, "will set you free."

The foundation for this way of thinking goes right back to the Old Testament.

When Moses is at the burning bush God speaks to him and says that he should go to Pharaoh and tell him to, "Let my people go." Moses was actually a fairly timid soul, who stuttered, and was unsure. To quote Exodus, "Moses said to God, 'Suppose I go to the Israelites and say to them, 'The God of your fathers has sent me to you,' and they ask me, 'What is his name?' Then what shall I tell them?"[12]

He asks God for his 'name'.

In Jewish custom your name designated your nature – who you were in reality. It tells you what you can expect from that individual.

God could have said anything – "Tell them that it is the all powerful God that sends you," or "I am the fire that will reign down on you if my will is not done."

But he does not say that. Instead:

"God said to Moses, "I AM WHO I AM. This is what you are to say to the Israelites: 'I AM has sent me to you.'"[12]

"*I am* has sent you." That is pretty strange don't you think? That God would define himself as "I am".

What it really means is "Tell them that the very essence of who you are has sent you".

"I am" ultimately denotes our essence: I am a man, I am a father, I am a postman etc. The ultimate "I am" is that divine consciousness that we have spoken of. The supreme being that we are able to access through our consciousness.

God is saying to Moses – tell them that you come in the name of that supreme being that exists within you.

Once again we are being pointed towards the heart of who we are, and told that at that heart lies a "beingness" that connects all things.

And when you look at it, people are getting enlightened all over the Bible. What is the Burning Bush (shining light) but an enlightenment experience? Paul on the road to Damascus (shining light), Jesus at the Transfiguration (shining light again), or Elijah on the mountain-side (still small voice).

Wherever you look, there are people throughout the Bible having traditional, good old-fashioned enlightenment experiences.

It is as if Christianity should be considered as an "Eastern religion".

Aged 22 – "Police are looking for..."

I always fancied working at the BBC. So when I found myself driving past their premises off Whiteladies Road in Bristol, I just turned in and parked the car.

I wandered into the reception.

"Can I help you?"

"I'd like to work here."

"And who are you?"

"I'm a student at the University."

"Through these doors, down the stairs, and it's the office straight ahead of you."

So began my short career in broadcasting.

Jenni Murray presented the morning programme, Kate Adie was on the local TV news, and just about anyone could join in. Local Radio was open to all.

My first job was reporting on flooding at the Severn Beach. I was sent off to do the legwork with a reporter who was to do the reporting.

I ran around trying to find likely people to interview – someone who had their house flooded out, another person who had had his jaw wired together to lose weight (we reported anything we could).

After an hour or so we were to 'opt into' Jenni Murray's morning programme.

The reporter stood there with his headphones on listening intently while I had a fag.

Suddenly he began to look animated, and then he was off:

"I'm here at this scene of utter devastation....houses flooded.....jaws wired.... "

Eventually he came to an end; however, rather than handing back to the studio, he said, "And I'm here with our other reporter, Nicholas Vesey. Nicholas, how do you see the situation?" After which he handed me the microphone.

I was mid fag and miles away, but just began speaking. I strung words together that sort of made sense, however, forgot to breathe between the words, so I got to the point where, if I took a breath, it would sound more like I was coming up for air after being under the water for a couple of minutes.

The reporter saw my distress and revelled in it – That will teach you, you cocky little sod – I could see him thinking.

I frantically made a cutting motion across my neck, pleading with him to take the microphone as I ran out of breath. And just before I died he took it and continued as if nothing had happened.

When I heard that my friend had been offered a freelance contract for the holidays I was incensed. I wanted one. I asked to see the station manager, who asked me when I could start.

There was no training as such. You were just put on shifts, and if you couldn't "drive the desk" you had to get someone to show you how.

It was terrifying: rows of knobs and dials. Some put you on the air, some put "London" on the air.

Soon I was coming in at 6am and doing the "morning show". I was useless. I could never quite get over that fear of speaking at nothing. It seemed pointless. And I was always afraid. You could get tripped up by anything. Like having to read out the names of the Chinese cricket team during the news, or being asked to comment on something when you weren't ready.

After 7am was the drive-time programme, and if you were on "earlies" you had to operate the desk for the more complicated bits (cue long pauses as I opened the wrong microphone).

But there is nothing quite like the atmosphere of a radio station. The excitement when some real piece of news comes in and everything is put on standby. Or making up requests during a record programme, and marrying off your friends and giving them huge families: "This next record is for Duncan and Jayne on the birth of their third set of twins – all the best to you all."

Or the day when I received a chain letter through the post, and so as not to break the chain I photocopied the letter on the BBC machine and dropped them through letterboxes on an estate on the way home.

The next day I was editing in one of the studios while listening

to a live feed from the station. It was the last item on the news.
"And finally an old people's home in Bristol has called in the
police after 40 of its residents were thrown into panic by an
abusive chain letter that was put through their doors last night.
The letter threatened... police are looking for..."
Help.

Eventually my studies started to severely deteriorate and I was
called in by my head of Department.
"You're not doing enough work," he accused.
I blustered.
"You've got a job haven't you?"
I blustered some more (how things have changed, nowadays not
having a job would be the exception).
"No," I said. "Nothing like that."
"Don't lie to me, Vesey," he said. "I heard you reading the news
this morning."

The more you know, the less you understand

This sense of the supreme being at the centre of our identity goes
right back to the beginning of the Bible.

"Then God said, 'Let us make man in our image, in our
likeness, and let him rule over the fish of the sea and the birds of
the air, over the livestock, over all the earth, and over all the
creatures that move along the ground.' So God created man in
his own image, in the image of God he created him; male and
female he created them."[12]

The idea that God created man in his own image, or in his
own "likeness", clearly suggests that God put something of
himself in humanity. That we are of the same nature of God in
some aspects, as well as being human.

You can see the whole story of the Bible as being the story of our emergence into consciousness; of that divine essence that is at the centre of our consciousness.

Here is a summation of the story in the Bible:

Eden
Fall
Slavery /Exodus
Wisdom
Prophets
Jesus Coming
Jesus Come
Jesus Overcomes Death
Jesus To Return

If you look at those topics from a perspective of one's individual consciousness, they work out as follows:

Eden

The original state of "unknowingness". Being united with that divine consciousness in the womb and as a little child, but not knowing it.

The fall from grace

Loss of Innocence – "I'm not perfect." We realise that we are out in the big, bad world, and our mind does all it can to keep us alive and surviving – sometimes too successfully.

Slavery

Mechanistic living – our mind and our senses take over. Virtually all our actions come about as a result of a stimulus/response mechanism orchestrated by the mind and the senses. We respond and react based upon past experience.

Exodus

The time when Moses led the Israelites out of Egypt, representing our beginning to travel out of mechanistic living by seeing that we are not our minds, but that there is something greater than us that contains us – a supreme being. The acknowledgement of this supreme being changes our whole perception on life and the fact that the universe might be a friendly place after all.

Wisdom

The books of wisdom in the Bible, like Proverbs and the Psalms, represent the development of understanding. We now begin to see the implications of there being a supreme being, and start to make connections with the way that we live our lives.

Prophets

The prophetic books in the Bible, such as Isaiah and Daniel, represent the understanding of the potential of that supreme being in our lives. How it could affect the way we live, now and in the future.

Jesus Coming

The whole expectation that a Messiah would come, and the idea that Jesus would change things for everyone represents an expectation of a direct knowledge of God, or that supreme being. A gradual realisation that it is possible to experience that divine consciousness, through our own consciousness.

Jesus Come

Represents the actual having of that experience, or the ability to live as if that experience were a constant reality in our lives.

Jesus Overcomes Death

The idea of the resurrection, the coming back from the dead, is the idea that we can fully move out of "mechanistic living", and instead live in the freedom of the knowledge that we are supported and looked after by a friendly universe.

Jesus to Return

The idea of the second coming represents our return to that state of grace that we were born with. Being able to live in the innocence of a supported environment that completely cares for us, such as the womb. We live our lives without thought for the future or the past, just enjoying the presence of our lives supported by that supreme being.

The Bible can be seen on a macro level and a micro level:

On a macro level it is the way that humanity has struggled with the idea of a supreme being: The stories it has been inspired to tell about that being, the ways that different cultures have related to each other, seemingly moderated by the same supreme being; leading to a development of understanding that goes from animal sacrifice and the laying down of laws, to "love" being the only law.

On a micro level it shows how each of us individually moves through the same journey: The infantile battles and wars that children get involved it – their cruelty and their lack of compassion, as well as their desire to do the right thing and please authority figures in their lives. Then the rebellion of adolescence and the growing into maturity that enables us to form relationships built on love, and to embrace the self-giving that this love demands.

The Judeo-Christian story contains all the same elements as do the other great faith traditions. All of them are trying to moderate and understand the depth of consciousness that is available to us all.

They attempt to understand the reality that they discover – one that does not depend on their beliefs, but which informs those beliefs from experience.

And the experience which is written down by each tradition and used as scripture, or sacred writings.

One more poem from the Tao Te Ching to finish this section: number 47:[9]

Without opening the door,
you can open your heart to the world.
Without looking out your window,
you can see the essence of the Tao.

The more you know,
the less you understand

The Master arrives without leaving,
sees the light without looking,
achieves without doing a thing.

Chapter 5

Past, Present and Future

Aged 6 – "Familia contra mundum"

At night we lay in our beds, hearing our mother crying downstairs. When I asked her what the matter was she simply said, "Grown-up worries."

Grown-up worries.

It's what you get when your husband dies of a cerebral haemorrhage leaving you with one son six weeks old and the other 18 months.

Two children minus one husband adds up to a whole lot of difficulty.

And it was not much better for my brother and myself, each of us desperate to get our mother's attention. And boy did we do our best to do that.

We had an old Mini-Minor, actually the first red Mini in Camberley, or so the family legend has it.

My mother parked it on the driveway outside the garage.

I managed to find the nails by clambering on to a chair and then up on to the workbench. They looked huge to me, although thinking back on it they were probably only 4 or 6 inches long.

I carefully took eight of them out of the brown paper bag and brought them to the car.

I took them two at a time and rested them against each of the tyres, front and back.

The way I saw it the car would roll back on to the nails and "pop".

I can't remember why the plan failed, but it did. I can't even remember if I was punished.

My fire was more successful.

I found some of that straw which came in wooden tea chests. It was more like wood shavings than straw, however, definitely flammable.

I made a pile of it by the garage door and lit it. Goodness knows where I got the matches.

It can't have done much damage, because the garage was still there when we left the house. Again I cannot remember any punishment, but there must have been one.

I once found some snow in a rubber bucket, again high up in the garage – I needed a chair to get to it.

At least I thought it was snow, even though it was now nearly spring.

It turned out that it was sodium chlorate, and my mother was two frightened to punish me as we all ended up in hospital trying to get rid of the stuff.

Most of the fun things we did involved clambering.

Clambering on to the roof of the car, only to slide down and have the flesh taken off my kneecaps by the metal bumper.

Or the night when my mother was invited to dinner at the house opposite. We were left asleep with a babysitter downstairs.

Halfway through the main course across the road, one of the guests pointed out of the open window towards our house.

"Mrs Vesey," he said, "aren't those your children on the flat roof of your house over there?"

And it was: Us on the roof with the babysitter asleep downstairs.

We did not have an unhappy childhood.

Outwardly it was all rushing up and down the road on bikes and playing cowboys and Indians with the other army boy down the road. There was an old retired General who used to provide some sort of father figure for us: letting us use his flame thrower and explore some of life through a man's eyes.

He later became Governor of Guernsey.

My mother did the best she could in the circumstances. We had good Christmases and birthdays. We had a sense of family, in the "familia contra mundum" way of operating, however, what all three of us lacked was love.

It was no one's fault, but I never learned how to give and receive love. The warmth of arms enfolded in comfort. The peace of a heart quietly beating close to one's own. Care given, and care received.

For years I never knew I was missing anything. I thought everyone else had the same experience as me. It just seemed that other people were better adjusted than me, and I could not work out why. Instead, life was a battle; something that involved victory or defeat. With victory came plunder and reward. With defeat came shame and ignominy.

In the end I lost my family and it would be years before I could find my way back to them again. Love finally brought me back, and we now share something special between us.

What has happened to us to shape us into the people we are today?

It is all very well discussing enlightenment, divine consciousness and all the other related things that we have gone through in this book so far, but if it does not have an effect on the way we live our lives, we might as well be discussing a painting or a film – interesting, but not necessarily life changing.

What is important is the personal transformation that brings about the changes that will really make a difference to the way we experience life.

The purpose of developing consciousness is to enable us to live our lives more skilfully. To improve the quality of our lives, and to enable us to make a greater contribution to the life that is around us. The less we worry about our own lives, the more time we have to give to others.

And if you define wealth as "the ability to give", that is no bad thing.

A part of developing our consciousness must therefore be to look at the way we have lived our lives up to now. What has happened to us to shape us into the people we are today? Many of us have done this before; however, to some of us it is completely new territory. I am just going to give you an opportunity to take a look at the journey that your life has taken, and reflect on where you are at the moment.

If you would like to take an inventory of your life so far, write a list of the key events in your life, the ones that have shaped you. Not only the events that you would consider "spiritual", but ones that have affected the essence of who you are, and therefore your spirit.

Once you've done that, choose 7 *key* events from your life.

Then draw a symbol for each of the events. For example the death of a parent could be a gravestone, or getting married a ring.

Finally, on a blank page use all the symbols to create an image that represents your life up to this moment.

There is no particular order or size to make any one of the symbols, just do what comes naturally to you. Use colours if you have them to hand to give the picture a more vivid feel.

Some of you may find this more difficult than others. Up to now all the work we have done has been rational thinking work. It is also good to explore using a more intuitive approach.

All of this is simply more developing of consciousness. This time developing consciousness on our past; on the way our life has developed, on what has made us the person we are.

When you have done that, take a look at the image you have made and see what it tells you about the way you view your life. If you feel you are able, show the image to someone else and tell them what it means to you.

Pain is our body's way of telling us that something is wrong

Looking at our past will inform our personal transformation, but not necessarily affect it.

Just making the shift from thinking that we are separate from the rest of life, to knowing that we are connected, makes a huge difference. It is moving from a dualistic view of life (me and the world), to a non-dual view of the world (we are all connected). But there is more.

Traditionally, personal transformation has been seen along moral grounds: I was a bad person, now I am a good person. I used to do bad things, now I do not do bad things.

In the Christian religion the preachers are always shouting, "Repent!"

Actually it is an interesting word; it is a translation of the Greek word "Metanoia", which means "to change one's mind". Not in the "I think I'd now prefer this orange to that apple" way of thinking. More like "I am going to replace the operating system on my computer" way of thinking.

Metanoia is about changing the way our mind thinks: From thinking that we are separate, to knowing that we are all connected via a supportive supreme being.

How you navigate your way through that change is more difficult.

It is fine to say, "Right, I acknowledge the existence of a divine reality, and I know I am a part of it," but most of the time we just keep on doing the things that we have always done, because that is the way we have learned to live our lives.

Preachers will talk about sin and giving up all the bad things that we are doing. But that does not really change anything. The feelings come back and we just bottle them up. Eventually something must give, and it normally does.

(Sin is also an interesting word. It does not mean those things we do that we know are bad, it actually means turning away from the natural care offered by the friendly universe (i.e. God) and trying to make yourself happy on your own – not easy, and usually expensive.)

For me pain is much more the issue.

People do not go down to the pub and throw back ten pints of larger just for the hell of it. A lot of the time it is to get rid of pain. It is the same with drugs – many people take drugs as a form of self-medication – again, often, to get rid of pain. That was the case for me.

Actually, I never even realised I was in pain; I thought everyone felt the same way I did. I just could not figure out why others seemed to have an easier time of it.

Most of us are so used to pain that we do not realise we are experiencing it.

We have spent our lives developing coping mechanisms to minimise the pain, so that it has become minimal, and therefore we do not register it.

What we *do* register is that we drink a lot, or we take a lot of drugs, or we sleep around, we eat a lot, or we are very driven in our careers, or we do not let others come too close, or we just hide away, or .... Fill in the blank for your own coping mechanism.

The bad news is that in order to be able to transform, we have got to become conscious of the pain that we have spent years trying to get rid of.

Because pain is our body's way of telling us that something is wrong.

You step on a pin, and your body says, "Hey, mind that pin."

You put your hand near a flame, "Watch that – it might do you harm."

The pain in your leg tells you that you have pulled a muscle.

The one in your hip tells you that the joint has worn out... and so on.

It is the same with emotional pain. It is saying, "Deal with this, please." But we don't; we try to make the pain go away. We avoid the pain through coping mechanisms rather than allowing it to tell us exactly what is wrong.

Khalil Gibran in his wonderful book *The Prophet* [13] (which, like the Tao Te Ching, is written in short stanzas) speaks about pain:

And a woman spoke, saying, "Tell us of Pain."
And he said:
"Your pain is the breaking of the shell that encloses your under-standing.
Even as the stone of the fruit must break, that its heart may stand in the sun, so must you know pain.
And could you keep your heart in wonder at the daily miracles of your life, your pain would not seem less wondrous than your joy;
And you would accept the seasons of your heart, even as you have always accepted the seasons that pass over your fields.
And you would watch with serenity through the winters of your grief.
Much of your pain is self-chosen.
It is the bitter potion by which the physician within you heals your sick self.
Therefore trust the physician, and drink his remedy in silence and tranquillity:
For his hand, though heavy and hard, is guided by the tender hand of the Unseen,

And the cup he brings, though it burn your lips, has been fashioned of the clay which the Potter has moistened with His own sacred tears."

Your pain tells us the exact place where you need to transform. That part of you that you have tried to get rid of is the very thing that will enable you to move on.

I am not saying that you should not take medication, or that when you have an operation you should not have an anaesthetic. Nor am I saying that you should just suffer if you have a problem. You should get help.

What I am saying is that many of us have emotional pain that we carry around with us and refuse to acknowledge – pain around loss, or hurt, or loneliness, or love, or disappointment – whatever it is for you.

We need to acknowledge that pain, and the coping mechanisms we have developed, and see where experiencing that pain will lead us.

Aged 16 – "Nothing has really been healed"

They say that the average man thinks about sex every seven seconds. Schoolboys think about it even more.
At the boarding school I went to there was no obvious homosexuality, just acres of porn. It was everywhere. People went out to the local shops and brought it back and traded it; there were stories of boys who met local girls in the woods; and then there were the dormitory dances. On the outside these were opportunities, organised by the staff, for boys living in a same sex school to meet girls, who also lived in same sex schools, and find out how the other half lived.
In reality they were a chance to try out sexual fantasies.

We would all congregate in the music school where someone was putting on records. After a while the girls would be brought in. We had never met them before. We circled each other and gradually paired off.

After a bit of dancing the boy would say, "Do you fancy going for a walk?" and off you would go.

Into one of the music practice rooms, outside into the rhododendron bushes, anywhere that gave you the privacy to live out that fantasy for an hour or so, and then store it up in the memory to be replayed over and over again in the months to come.

The girls were as keen as the boys, but it never went "all the way".

Sex was the main aim of parties, and that continued after you had left school.

If you were organising a party in someone's home you always had a room for dancing, a room for drinks, a room for chatting and a room for sex, normally with mattresses on the floor to make it more comfortable.

Most people grew out of it in their early twenties. They formed relationships and had no real need for grubbing around on the floor with a stranger at a party.

I never grew out of it. I think mostly because afterwards I always felt such revulsion, both for myself and for the other person. I just wanted to get away from them, and that meant I had to start all over again.

It did not seem to be about relating, more about release. As if this was the only way for the pain to go away, if only for a short time. Then you were left with the physicality of it all: the mess, the humiliation, and this other person that had seen you in that way. Without the warmth of affection there was only the coldness of being alone, with someone else. That was certainly no basis for relating, and yet I could see no other way through.

I yearned for love. While others planned careers and fantasised about being rich, powerful and or famous, I just wanted love.

I wanted that warmth that others seemed to feel; that intimacy that they shared with each other. Every time I sought it I got nowhere. I was in complete poverty as far as love went, and became determined to make myself rich.

Many years later, when parties were no longer about sex, and you just did not know enough people who would be willing to sleep with you, there were the massages.

I would suddenly get an all consuming urge to be touched, and with it a thought that this form of naked intimacy was the only one that could satisfy the pain.

As the thought grew, so the pain grew, and it just had to be dealt with.

They were like shops, with a little sign in the window that said "Sauna and massage". You checked the street to make sure that you were not being observed in your humiliation, and then rang the bell.

It was quickly answered (they understood that you did not like to be kept waiting on the street) by a woman, usually in her thirties who had presumably graduated from massages to being on reception.

"Hello, dear, fancy a massage? Sign in here." For some reason I always used my own name. "Linda will take you today."

And Linda would appear and take you to a small room with what looked like a doctor's couch, where you took off your clothes and put on a towel.

You lay on the couch on your front and the massage started. At last, someone was touching you.

Eventually the pain is released and you are back on the street, £60 lighter and with a sense that nothing has really been healed.

A pair of fives is a winning hand

We all have great needs, but from a spiritual perspective, we want for nothing.

Materially we might need water or food or other things which, if withdrawn from us, will cause us to die. But from a spiritual perspective, there is always abundance.

Right now, as you read this book, you lack nothing. You lack no insight, no knowledge, no realization – it is all there and available to you.

Because *this* is it. *This* is all there is.

How could there be any more?

You have everything you need to make the perfect next step in your life; to solve that sticky relationship that you have always been struggling with; to experience complete union with the divine essence of life.

The only trouble is that we do not believe it. We think that if only I understood this thing, or did not have that pain, or could travel to this place, then everything would be perfect.

Not true. You have it all now. Eckhart Tollë spends a whole book looking at *The Power of Now*,[11] and it is all there.

We think we have to change. We think we have to be different in order to become whole, to become healed, but we do not.

Each of us has been dealt a hand in our lives, and most of us spend our lives trying to throw in the hand we were given, and get another one.

The thing we never figure out is the fact that the game is fixed. We might only have been dealt a pair of fives, however, in the game we are playing a pair of fives is a winning hand. Because the game is set by the same "friendly universe" as dealt us our hands in the first place.

We look at what others have, and we say – "If only I had wealth and fame, then I would be able to have everything I wanted."

And yet that is almost always not true.

You might have been given a hand where the ultimate spiritual and emotional fulfilment in your life comes from being exactly who you are and where you are.

In fact you are the *only* person who would be able to be content in the situation that you are in, because that is how life works.

I am not saying that one should not strive to get on and achieve, to go for excellence, and generally to try and make the best out of our lives. We should all do that. What I am saying is that we should play to the hand we have been dealt, knowing and trusting that it is a winning hand, and if we play it correctly we will get our heart's desire.

I am also not saying that we should not fight to get out of situations that are not supportive, where we get hurt and abused. We should always try to improve our lot. What I am saying is that we do not have to be somebody else in order to make that happen. We have the means within ourselves.

Part of understanding that there *is* a divine consciousness that underpins all life is the fact that you can trust life. You can trust *your* life.

No one else has lived life the way you have. You have a completely unique relationship with that life; with the divine consciousness that has given you birth, with the people and the things that you have connected with, and with circumstances and situations that you are involved with.

Everything in your life has brought you to this moment right now.

Right now.

All the good ideas, all the relationships, all the learning, all the money, everything you have ever done has brought you to this moment now, reading this book, this chapter, this page, this line, this word... now.

Your whole future lies in front of you and your past lies behind you.

You are here, right now.

And it will never get any better than this, or any worse. It will just be different. Whether you think that difference is better or worse will be a judgement that your mind will make at some point in the future, but outside that – it will just be what it is – right now.

As Khalil Gibran says, *"And you would accept the seasons of your heart, even as you have always accepted the seasons that pass over your fields. And you would watch with serenity through the winters of your grief."*

It is all here and available, right now. The rest is what you think about it.

Real transformation comes when you see "what is" for what it is. That pain is just pain, and joy is joy. They are different. It is about wanting what you get, rather than trying to get what you want. And when you do that you trust life. You trust the hand you have been dealt. You trust your ability to play that hand, and you make no prejudgements about the way the game is going. *You* are not running the game; life is running it.

Work with your life and you have everything you need. The moment you try to take over the game, to change your hand, to change the game, you are lost – because it is not your game, you are a part of a bigger game being played by life.

Aged 21 – "I'll show you a trick"

Mombasa was full of prostitutes.

As a young white man walking down the street in the evening you are propositioned every ten yards. Peter and I never considered accepting.

Our room was a small dormitory of 8 beds. It was a hovel costing a few shillings a night, but that was all we had.

Lying in bed that night I was woken up by a strange clack... clack... clack... sound.

I turned on the light and the source was immediately obvious.

All around there were hundreds of cockroaches climbing up the walls. When they got to a certain height they no longer had the strength to hold on, and they fell backwards on to the wooden floor with a clack, only to crawl back to the wall and start again.

In the morning we took the bus for Tiwi Beach. They dropped us at the side of the road and pointed into the jungle – one mile that way.

We walked for about half an hour and eventually hit the beach, deserted but for a couple of Swedes who had been living there for a year. Not a building in sight.

We stayed two days in our tents, living off the odd bit of fruit we had brought with us and what we could scrounge from the Swedes.

I have always thought that desert island living was overrated, and this proved it to me. Yes it was beautiful, but with no showers, sand mites biting you everywhere, and no morning coffee we quickly decided that enough was enough and headed for home.

Home was Nairobi, nearly 300 miles away. The only problem was that we had run out of money. And not just down to our last $20. We were completely flat broke.

We had to hitch.

I stood at the side of the road and stuck out my thumb. After about 20 minutes a four door saloon stopped and offered us a lift. It turned out he was a Nigerian civil servant, however, he was only going the first fifty miles along the road, and he dropped us at a small village before turning off.

We were desperate for a drink. So the only thing to do was to open our bags and try to sell what we had left – our clothes.

A crowd quickly formed around us. No one spoke English. Apparently I was being offered a small calf in exchange for my favourite red jacket.

Eventually we managed to barter the jacket for a couple of cokes, and began hitching again.

An old Land Rover stopped and offered us a lift. We got in the back and threw ourselves on to the floor and slept.

After some time the car stopped and our driver came round the back and opened the tailgate.

"We need new tyres, and you pay."

We tried to explain to him that we had no money, but it was just not very convincing. Two affluent white young men, casually dressed, a bit rugged, but obviously well fed and with few worries, how could they have no money?

The conversation became more heated.

"You give money NOW."

"But really we haven't got any, honestly. We are extremely sorry… "

Eventually, after he had searched both us and our bags, he threw us off the car and drove away in disgust, leaving us at the side of the road. It was about 6pm and getting dark.

In Africa it is light, and then it is dark, very quickly. The last thing we wanted to do was to be caught out at night.

About a mile ahead was a truck stop. We made for it.

When I say truck stop what I really mean is a corrugated iron shed surrounded by about fifty trucks.

We walked to the shed and opened the door. It was a bar full of drivers and the odd woman. As we opened the door the rowdiness inside fell into silence with a "Hurrrrrubbbbleaaaaaaaaaaa."

All eyes turned to us. The only white faces in the place.

I turned to Peter and told him to wait by the door as I walked to the bar.

Suddenly, all the lights in the place went out. In the darkness I felt three pairs of hands efficiently search me.

Presumably satisfied that I had no money or weapons the lights came back on again.

I was standing between two huge men. Everyone was looking at me in silence.

I turned to the man on my left and said, "I'll show you a trick."
It was all I could think of.

I had learnt the trick in a bar a few years previously. It involved putting ash on someone's hand, and then mysteriously having the ash move from one hand to another. I had been fascinated by it and had eventually persuaded the person to tell me how to do it.

He made me swear to keep the secret and then said it would save my life one day.

That day seemed to have come.

"Put your hands out in front of you," I said to the man. He did so, and I began.

Palms up, apply the cigarette ash to the palm, clench both fists. Open them, palms down. Rub the palms on the trouser leg. Palms up. Clench fists. The confusion spread on the man's face.
"Which hand did I put the ash on?" I asked.

"This one," said the trucker.

"Now look at the other one." The driver opened the other hand, and there was the ash.

There was uproar, everyone shouting at the same time.

After a while my driver motioned for quiet.

"Shhh Shhhh," he said, and fixed me with his eyes as the bar went quiet again.

"Was that bush or was that medicine?" he asked.

Now, I knew that much depended on my answer – we were about fifty miles from Nairobi, at night, in the middle of nowhere – and I had not a clue what to say.

To this day I cannot remember which answer I gave, but it must have been the right one for the whole bar erupted again in a huge cheer.

My driver clapped me on the back and shouted:

"Good man, I take you to Nairobi."

And so he did.

Just take the next step, and then the one after that

So we have come down to the essence of what it means to be developing consciousness. It is to be aware of all that is going on around us – our thoughts and feelings, our senses and the way our reality comes together.

To be aware of our past and what has shaped us to become the person that we are.

To be aware of being conscious of all those things, and realising that there is a deeper consciousness that is accessible to all, and that we all share.

That divine consciousness gives us life; it gives us our ability to sense, think and to act; it frames the game that we play in.

The choice we have in life is whether or not we participate with that consciousness, or we try to make up our *own* game and play that.

If the universe is a friendly place, and if we are given all that we need to be fully satisfied, then living skilfully is really just sensing what life is trying to tell us, and then acting in conjunction with the game that has been set up for us.

All of which does not preclude the existence of less friendly influences on our lives.

The best definition of "evil" that I have come across is "the privatisation of good".

When someone or something tries to take a "good" for him or herself, then evil is being done.

Rape is an example, where a "good" is being forcibly taken by someone; it is not being given.

The holocaust is an example of Nazi Germany attempting to take a good for itself, and in so doing destroying all in its path.

I like this definition because it defines evil in terms of good, saying that good is the basic raw material in the world, and that there are some who will not accept this, so instead they feel the need to take it; to start their own game with their own rules.

Surely that is madness. To think that we can understand life in such a way that we can control it does not show sanity. Life is infinitely more complicated than we can ever imagine, and so the only way to play the game of life is to discover what the ultimate rules are, not to try and dictate the rules ourselves in an attempt to beat the system.

It is interesting to notice that some of the wealthiest men in the world gradually turn mad on the issue of control.

Howard Hughes could control anything he wanted, except microbes, and that is what got him. He ended up isolated, padding around his room on tissue paper, terrified that he would be contaminated in some way. That is the logical extension of trying to control the game of life. Life is already in control, our free will is to decide whether or not we co-operate with it.

So the rest of story is really about the nature of that co-operation.

How do you engage with that which is at the seat of our being in such a way as to make the most out of our lives?

Is there a way of being that lends itself to that co-operation?

This is a dangerous area, because it is out of this question that religions are formed.

Someone thinks they know the way, or the interpretation of the way that some great teacher had supposedly laid down years before, and they declare that, "This is The Way, folks!" Such action has nothing to do with developing consciousness.

I have nothing against religions, they provide a context for growth and development and employment; however, what we are talking about here is our own unique life with its own unique hand and its own unique set of circumstances.

Only *you* will know the right way to go, based upon what you know. And, let's face it, you know it all. No one else is as well briefed on your life as you are. No one else knows all the ins and outs of your life like you do. After all, you are the one who has lived it. Don't let anyone persuade you that they know better what to do than you do.

You are the one who has to hear the still small voice that comes after your storm. You are the one that sees what you see and hears what you hear. The trick is to be responsible for that; to credit what you see and hear as being important for you. That it is not just any old life; it is *your* life with all its uniqueness. And you are the one who has all that you need to see yourself safely through to the other side (so to speak).

All that follows now is ways that you can do that more skilfully (back to that). Ways that enable you to develop and grow and sense what to do next.

Because that is all that you have to do in this life: Just take the next step, and then the one after that.

Aged 25 – "They have seen you at your worst"

There were about fifty people around me sitting in chairs, about eight rows deep, in theatre style with an aisle down the middle.
We all had our eyes shut and were making a sound, "Ahhhhhhhhhh."
It had begun three days ago in the Great Western Royal Hotel in Paddington; in their Devon Room to be exact. One of thousands of conference facilities all over London that were rented out to whoever had the money.
In this case it was to a self-awareness seminar that I had enrolled in run by The Exegesis Programme.
My life was out of control, and I needed to find some way of getting a handle on it. This seemed as good as any. Three days of intensity. They didn't tell you what would happen, just that you could transform your life in those three days.
On the first day they took away our watches and read us the ground rules.
We were not to speak unless we put our hands up; we were never

to be late, we had to write in our notebooks at every break, and never address any members of staff – unless in the seminar room. There was a lot of shouting: People were late, they got shouted at; they left their notebooks in the seminar room; more shouting. Anything that infringed any ground rule incurred the accusation that we were "fucking assholes" and that our lives "did not work."

This went on for 9 hours.

We started at 9am in the morning and the first meal break was at 6pm.

Exhausted, we fell out of the hotel into the chaos of the rush hour on Praed Street. We stuffed ourselves with revolting food and were back in the room, ready to begin at 7.30.

Gradually we began to tow the line. We all made less mistakes, and began to look at the state of our lives. We participated by asking questions and sharing experiences; we listened to the lives of others and we started to get the hang of it.

The first day finished at 2.00am, and we were back in our seats ready to begin at 9am the next day.

Day two was about our inhibitions. We played animated charades where we got shouted at if we did not put 100% into the exercise. People broke down in tears and "pushed through". Quiet people were made to be loud, butch people were made to be effeminate, and girly girls were made to act like stomping giants. By the end we did not know who we were.

Then we were put into "catharsis": 50 people, all lying on the floor conjuring up their worst nightmares and screaming their heads off. Goodness knows what the other hotel guests made of it. Some became so hysterical that their arms curled up and they went into spasms.

Eventually we were allowed out for supper. It was 6.30, nine and a half hours without food.

When we came back we were made to line up like prisoners and marched into the room to much shouting –"No talking!", 'Stand in line!"

In front of us was a platform. "All your patheticness will now be revealed."

In groups of six we were marched up on to the platform and told to, "Let it all go."

One by one those on the platform began to cry or scream. "Let go," they shouted at us, and we did. The screams got louder the tears more intense.

After about 5 minutes the hysteria subsided and the group was left panting on the stage. Six assistants then arrived, and one stood directly in front of each of the participants. "Be with them, they have seen you at your worst, now see that you are OK, nothing has happened to you, there is no judgement in their eyes. You are OK, just be with it."

That group was then marched off the stage, and the next went up. This group knew what was coming and were even more scared.

On the last day it was all smiles; you could talk to the assistants and they would talk to you. It was as if you had passed the initiation and you now knew that everyone had all that fear and grief inside them, and that it was OK. Something had moved inside us.

The day was about possibilities. What could you do with your life if you were not afraid?

At the end of the day we were asked to close our eyes and imagine a perfect beach. Flute music came out of a sound system. "Now people your beach with the kind of people you would like to have in your life." We were then asked to make the noise.

"Ahhhhhhhhh."

"Louder."

"AHHHHHHHHH."

"Louder."

"AHHHHHHHHHHHHHHHHHHHHHHHHH."

Suddenly the noise reached a crescendo and burst into cheers and applause. I opened my eyes and the room was filled with people, about 200, all cheering and clapping. They had appeared out of nowhere; apparently past participants of the seminar, graduating our new group.

I felt ecstatic. It was as if all constraints had been lifted from my life. None of the old rules applied. All the walls had come down, all the ropes and chains had been broken and all the burdens had been lifted off my life. The doors were open and I was free.

Free at last. Free, and a new person.

I stood and rushed up to the person standing nearest me and hugged them. I did not stop hugging people for the next half an hour.

In fact I am still hugging people to this day.

I had left the past behind.

Books fall off shelves

The way we develop our relationship with the essence of life is what people call a spiritual practice.

It is just the process of practising the skill of making a connection with that essence.

Anything can take the form of spiritual practice: Reading this book is a form of spiritual practice – you are taking the ideas and experiences that it generates and using them as a reference point for reflecting on your relationship with life.

It helps to take on some form of practice for all this stuff to have any meaning.

It is like being on a sailing ship out at sea.

The ship will simply bob around on the water until you put some sails up. The moment you do that the wind catches the sails and you begin to move. In extreme circumstances a ship might be caught by a storm and driven along without any sails, and in life some people do get sudden realisations seemingly coming out of nowhere, but in general it is through our practice that our life speaks to us.

We have to trust where the wind takes us. That old saying that a rich man is less likely to enter the kingdom of heaven than a camel going through the eye of the needle is true because many of us do not trust where we are being led.

It is as if we are in our sailing ship and the wind is taking us away from the comfort of the shore and out to sea. We go with it for a while, and then we have second thoughts.

Sneakily we have all installed engines into our ships, so that when the wind is taking us somewhere we do not want to go, we just turn on the engine and steer in the opposite direction.

In life that would be the equivalent of a rich man not liking the direction his life is taking, so he goes to the building society, draws out £10,000, and changes direction. If you are not rich, you cannot make such changes.

Our spiritual practice is what we do to enable that divine consciousness to enrich our lives. Any activity can take the form of a spiritual practice, so long as you have decided that you are going to use it for such a purpose: Going for a walk and being aware of what you feel and what you think; painting a picture; sitting in silence; reading a book; doing the garden, even doing the washing up.

It is us giving that divine consciousness "house room" in our lives. Sometimes, like a storm, that consciousness will just come upon us spontaneously; maybe in nature, or in conversation with a friend, or during sex, or while we are being creative, or while playing sport or during work: suddenly you begin to feel a sense of awe and wonder at the fact that you are a part of something that is greater.

Sometimes we set up circumstances to make that happen – our practice. It could be meditation, or chanting, or dance, or prayer, or any of the other things I have mentioned. In those cases we are deliberately saying, "I am setting aside this time to enable that essence of life to come through to me more powerfully." And you go about your practice.

When adopting a spiritual practice it should be one that suits you. The moment you begin to consider doing it, you will start to have ideas. Trust those ideas; they are coming to you from your own consciousness. That is the beauty of the system – the moment you begin to put your attention on co-operating with life, the moment you start responding to the desire to know that divine consciousness that is deep inside you, it begins to cooperate with you. You begin to get ideas, books fall off shelves, you meet people, see films, all of which magically seem to be leading you in the right direction. You are calling to your life and, like Mole's home in the *Wind in the Willows*, it will call back to you. It will lead you home. It is then that your "two fives" becomes a winning hand, because there is no greater wealth than to be in contact with the source of our lives. It will feed us and nurture us in ways that we cannot even imagine.

Aged 25 – So you open another bottle to find your inspiration

I was bored working in advertising.
Masius Wynne Williams was one of the big agencies, but it was not the most glamorous; my job as a lowly junior account manager was most definitely the bottom rung of the ladder.
I wanted to be a copywriter. They came in at 10 in the morning, wore jeans and left whenever they wanted.
I asked the personnel department of the Agency, but they just laughed.
One morning I was driving in to work in St James's Square when I heard an ad for a competition on Capital Radio. The prize was a job in a top agency as a copywriter.

I decided to enter.

The competition, however, was for students, so I made no mention of my job.

I wrote an ad about getting people to use bicycles more, and sent it in.

Eventually I was shortlisted, interviewed, and to cut a long story short, ended up as a copywriter at Foote Cone and Belding, another big agency.

The thing about creative people in advertising (that's the Art Directors and Copywriters who actually think up the ads) is that they are often not actually advertising products to customers. What they are really doing is advertising themselves to their colleagues. "You're only as good as your last ad", and so you want to make sure that everyone thinks your last ad was a good one.

That's what awards are for, and advertising is big on awards; they tell the rest of the industry that you've done good work.

Now I am sure this is not the case for the real pros, but for us struggling juniors it sure looked liked the way things worked.

So, the whole idea was to get into the best agency and do work that everyone else thought was fab.

It was an all-consuming occupation. You had to be completely focused in making sure that the best people saw your ads, and hired you.

Which is why my art director and I soon decided that FCB was not the place to be. Saatchi and Saatchi was the goal.

So we set about getting a portfolio and hawking it around the creative directors.

Eventually we got to Saatchi's, and miracle upon miracles, they offered us a contract.

"I suppose it would not make any difference if I doubled your salary," said the creative director at FCB. No it would not.

Creative people in advertising have a great time, so long as they produce.

"We want a campaign that says this. It needs that sort of a feel and we want ads for press, TV and posters."

You would then go away and think about it. Argue with your partner as to what was "shit", what had been done before, what others would approve of, and what they would not. The pressure was to get good and to stay that way as long as you could before you burnt out. "When was the last time you saw a copywriter over the age of 35?" people said to each other. And so we all got on the treadmill. Admittedly it was a treadmill that could end up with fast cars, international acclaim and million dollar bonuses, but it was still a treadmill. One ad after another.

If it came easily it was a breeze. You saw people who just came in, sat down and wrote brilliant work. For others it took hours of honing – 99% perspiration and 1% inspiration. Others drank their way to creativity, and still more took drugs. Dope, coke, whatever produced the work. The problem comes when you try to think up your next ad and you remember that the last time you did something really good it was after half a bottle of scotch. So you open another bottle to find your inspiration. It's called creative addiction, and it goes right across the creative arts, most obviously in the music business. It always ends in tears.

I did not last very long at Saatchi's; there was just too much pressure, and I was not quite good enough. I was certainly not as good at it as my art director who went on to run his own agency.

Getting out saved me from the worst excesses of myself.

One of the last commercials I wrote was for Godfrey Davis car rental. It was a 30 second series of comedy radio spots. The client had approved the scripts and we were casting.

The Creative Director of the Agency, Jeremy Sinclair, wanted an established broadcaster who worked on the Today Programme on Radio 4. I wanted an alternative comedian I had seen on the circuit.

Eventually I tested both of them and took the results to Jeremy.

"We'll go with the Radio 4 guy," he said. "We need someone well known. No one has ever heard of this other guy – what's his name?"

Rowan Atkinson.

The reward for sitting in silence, is sitting in silence

We cannot see what is right in front of us, that's why the journey involves trust.

I read somewhere the story of the Guru with the Pointing Finger.

There was once a guru who lived in some remote part of India and was famous for the way that he enlightened his students.

Every day they would congregate in the great hall for an audience. They would sit in silence and the guru would arrive and also sit in silence. After some time, always a different length of time, the guru would dramatically stand up and raise his arm to the horizontal with his index finger pointing upwards. He would hold that pose for a couple of minutes, and then leave the stage. The guru became famous because many of his pupils attained enlightenment.

One day a young man came to the ashram claiming that he wanted to join and to learn from the guru with the pointing finger. He was taken in and given a job in the kitchens.

After a few months the young man became disenchanted with the ashram. He began to fidget during the silences, and to make fun of the guru.

He would appear to groups of people and pretend to be the guru with the pointing finger, dramatically entering the library and copying the guru's movements, stretching out his arm and pointing his finger to the heavens.

One day he was doing this in the kitchen. He swept in and dramatically raised his arm and pointed up. Unbeknown to him the guru just happened to be in the kitchen at the time and he witnessed the charade.

The guru walked quickly across the room, picking up a sharp knife from the table as he went, and with one slash he severed the young man's index finger from his hand.

The young man screamed with pain and shock, clasping his bleeding hand and looking at the guru with bewilderment.

At which point the guru adopted his pose and raised his pointing finger towards the young man.

The young man was instantly enlightened.

What I like about this story is that the enlightenment comes out of nowhere. The young man is serious about his journey; the decision to join the ashram shows him to be so. Then, like all of us he becomes disenchanted with the journey. He feels that it is not producing results.

Consequently, his mind goes off on another journey, belittling his practice and using it to get attention. He plays the fool. Then, out of nowhere, the practice that he has embarked upon comes along and gives him such a shock that it throws his mind completely out of control. For a moment it cannot compute what is going on, and just at that moment the guru fixes the mind with the pointing finger, and it opens to the wonder of that enhanced consciousness.

This is how it can happen to us. Whatever we take on, we often become disenchanted. We think we are not getting anywhere and that it is not working. But we do not have the capacity to judge what is working and what is not working. All we can do is continue on the journey and trust that we are being led in the right direction.

And so we begin to see that the point of the spiritual journey is not the arrival, it is the journey itself.

As I said earlier, we have everything we need right now. The truth is that there is nowhere to go, no other experience to have. The journey is all there is.

Our life is that journey. In the end we do not arrive anywhere. We are born naked and with nothing, and we die naked and with nothing. All that there is in between is the journey. You either take that journey in co-operation with life, or you try to make your own way.

If you make your own way you have to decide where you are going, what you hope it will be like when you arrive, and then you plot your course.

The problem is that you can end up believing that life will only really begin when you have got to the place you want to arrive at.

The beauty of the spiritual journey is that the journey is all. To be on the journey is all that we hope for. It brings its own rewards, and you can never predict what they are going to be.

You do not hold out for the time that you are enlightened. You know that you already have everything, and you just let it unfold in front of you, realising that it is never going to be any better than it is right now.

And if you can get *that*, you are home and dry. If you can accept that that which you have now is all of it – and so you might as well enjoy it while you have got it – then you will always be rich.

The reward for sitting in silence is sitting in silence. The reward for mindfulness is mindfulness, the reward for knowing divine consciousness is that divine consciousness, it is as simple as that.

Take a while to sit and consider what you do as a form of spiritual practice. Then consider what you would like to take on for the future. In such a way you can structure the way you undertake your journey.

Aged 28 – "And finally.." the newsreader said at the end of the bulletin

I had never run an aircraft factory before, and was not much good at it.

We built Microlight Aircraft. All scaffolding poles, car seats, engines and propellers.

The SAS rang up one day and asked if they could look at one.

I was to meet them at Bristol airport.

When I arrived the security guard put me on a Land Rover and drove me out to the apron of the tarmac and told me to wait.

I looked around me – no one to be seen.

Suddenly a speck appeared in the sky in the distance, and soon the helicopter was gliding towards us.

It hovered about fifty feet away, and two army guys jumped out and ran towards me. The helicopter banked dramatically and headed for home.

"Right, we've got two hours," one of them said.

They tested the aircraft and exactly two hours later we were standing on the same piece of runway. The helicopter appeared as if by magic. They jumped on board and were gone.

Later they phoned and said that they would be willing to "test-destruct" the aircraft for us.

How much would they pay us?

"We have a policy of not paying for test work."

We had a policy of not delivering without payment.

That was the last we saw of them.

Later that winter it began to snow. Not many people buy Microlights in the winter, so the entire factory staff (all eight of us) were in the café opposite kicking our heels over mugs of tea. Then we had the idea. One that would surely generate enough PR to sell the five planes we had so far built (and failed to sell). I had a background in broadcasting, so I telephoned both the local television stations and told them that our planes were being used to feed sheep in this bad weather.

Neither station seemed very interested, but half an hour later we had a call.

"This is the newsroom of ITN in London. We are sending a cameraman to cover this story about Microlights and sheep. Where should he turn up?"

There was no farmer, no sheep, and certainly no plane feeding them... yet.

We gave them the address of the farm where we kept one of our test aircraft and then phoned the farmer. He was game.

Two hours later we had a plane, some bales of hay and a pilot. We saw a car drive up, and out of it stepped a fairly weedy-looking man with what looked to us like a "Super 8" film camera. It was tiny.

There was no "Local Farm Air Lift" going on. In fact we had yet to lift a bale of hay in anger. But the cameraman was not to know that.

What he did see was an extremely flimsy looking contraption that he was supposed to risk his life in for the sake of some stupid story.

We saw the panic spread across his face and decided to cut a deal. "Look," we said. "You don't want to fly all over the farm seeing all the sheep we've got. Why don't we just fly you from this field to that one, and you can film us chucking the hay out as if it were the real thing." The cameraman agreed with a visible sign of relief.

In the end he quite liked the flying and took a lot of film over the entire farm.

That evening we all sat down to watch the news, expecting to see ourselves in the "and finally" slot. However, as the theme music came on, so our pictures appeared.

The snow was the lead story, and ours the perfect vehicle for them.

"And finally..." the newsreader said at the end of the bulletin, "let's go back to that sheep rescue story and see some of the best aerial footage of the snow that we have seen so far. Goodnight."
And there we were again – on twice.
In the end we never sold any planes from the coverage. In fact the company went into receivership shortly afterwards.
However, a month later I received a letter from ITN which included a £30 cheque made out in my name.
The reason for the payment was put down on the paperwork as "reporter's fee".

A portal into another dimension

I began my spiritual practice with the Lord's Prayer, and I still use it to this day.

It is something that is mumbled all over the world. And yet for me it was like a portal into another dimension.

You can see it as a set of words that asks for different things in the hope that God will look after you. Or you can see it as a series of movement that unlocks an experience, like a combination lock, taking you into that other dimension.

It is interesting that when Jesus is asked to teach his disciples to pray, he does not go off into parables. He is quite specific, he says, "Go into your room, close the door and say this:

'Father of us,
The One who is in the heavens;
Hallowed be your nature
May your kingdom come,
May your will be done,
as in heaven, so on earth.
Give us today our bread from above that gives our whole life meaning.

Cancel our debts,
As we cancel the accounts of those indebted towards us.
And let us not be led into temptation,
but deliver us from evil.'"

I was given this translation by John Pettival, a Bible scholar, and it is the one I have used ever since.

The purpose of this set of words is to take us into the perfect attitude to accept the divine consciousness that is at the centre of all our lives. Each phrase deals with a different aspect of the way we look at our lives, and shapes us so that we are ready to come into the presence of "The eternal".

Father of us,
Acknowledges that the universe is a friendly place, that there is an "other" to relate to, and that other has a loving disposition towards us.

The One who is in the heavens;
Places that "other" in relationship to our lives. It is within us, it is all around us. Like a living sponge at the bottom of the sea-bed with the ocean in and around the creature.
So are we to that divine presence. It is in us and all around us.

Hallowed be your nature
Puts us in the correct relationship to that supreme being. Literally "may your being be regarded by me with a sense of respect and reverence". We acknowledge that all we can do in the presence of eternity is to bow down and give up to its magnificence.
May your kingdom come,
May your loving nature come to order all things. We give up to the wisdom and love that is present in the essence of that being, and allow it to order us and all that is around us.
May your will be done,

as in heaven, so on earth
Come and inhabit my life. May my life conform to your
purposes as I acknowledge that this game is yours, and I am
a part of that game. Wherever you are, you bring about
perfection, so bring perfection into my life.

*Give us today our bread from above that gives our whole life
meaning.*
Give meaning to my life – may I see my place in this bigger
picture and in so doing know what to do in any given
situation.

Cancel our debts,
As we cancel the accounts of those indebted towards us.
May I let go of any attachments I have in this life, and so be
able to focus on you. And in so doing may I let go of anything
that I am holding on to with regard to other people.

And let us not be led into temptation,
but deliver us from evil.
And may I not be put in situations where I feel the need to
choose between your way and my own way so that I may not
take to myself things that are not naturally given to me.

And then from the traditional form:

For the kingdom, the power and the glory are yours.
For everything I participate with in this life comes from you.
All power comes from you, and all thanks, for anything I
receive in this life, goes to you.

Now and forever
In this present moment which lasts for eternity.
Amen

So be it.

I have been using this set of words almost every day for the last 25 years and they always work.

They put you in exactly the right place to begin anything – silence, art, reading, writing. Whatever it is that you want to use as a practice, this is a perfect beginning point.

It takes you right through all the various stages that lead to an attitude of acceptance of what is so: Namely the existence of a supreme being; that this being is within us; that it is sacred; that we want it to consume us so that we will conform to its will; that we understand our place and its purpose for us; that we will leave behind all other attachments, and give ourselves fully into it; now and forever.

It is a mind-blowing journey of only a few short sentences, and it can transform your life.

It can also bring answers to problems. Sometimes I have been faced with something that I cannot work out, and I use this set of words and a solution miraculously appears. It seems to draw from somewhere very deep and shortcut our access to that divine consciousness.

Aged 25 – "Dressed in pink and carrying bendy rubber truncheons"

I had never been to Glastonbury Festival before. As I drove out of London I caught sight of a hitchhiker with a cardboard sign saying "Glastonbury". His lucky day.

We arrived on the Friday evening, parked the car, and walked to the festival site. It was huge and ranged down the hill to the pyramid stage where Steve Hillage was performing. I put up my tent and headed off.

In those days there were about 40,000 people on the site. It had the feel of a massive Camden Lock. As it got dark I wandered through the different areas, wood smoke constantly drifting around and joining with the ever present and sweet smell of dope.

Stalls mingled with tents and camp fires. There seemed to be no order to what you came across next.

The amazing thing was that everywhere you went you were welcomed with open arms. "Hey man, come and sit down – wanna smoke, have some tea."

When it was actually dark the camp fires lit the way. There were clowns performing in the circus big top, a film show in another tent, some folk singer in another.

The next morning the sun shone and I emerged to the wonderful sense of comradeship that seems to exist at a festival early in the morning.

People washing, pooing, doing their teeth and all with a bonhomie that was both welcoming and friendly. There was a tent frying eggs and bacon. People ate, drank real coffee and rolled joints. They were even selling a bootleg copy of Steve Hillage's set from the night before called Wreckage *on the* Hillside.

A sense of rightness and order prevailed around the place.

Over the whole weekend the only police I saw, or at least remember seeing, were dressed in pink and carrying bendy rubber truncheons. There was no trouble.

I wandered around in a kind of daze. It just seemed like one huge village where everyone was welcome.

I had never felt anything quite like it. There seemed to be a genuine sense of trust and brotherhood and I revelled in it, gradually shedding my cynical "London" attitude and adopting the same approach to those I met.

In the early afternoon someone put on We are Family *by Sister Sledge, and the whole crowd stood up to dance.*

Finally, just as the sun was going down John Martin came on.

He weaved such magic with his guitar and his voice that you truly felt you were in a special place.
Smoke hovered over the crowd as it sat and listened. One World.

By the end of his set I was completely satisfied.
I had met with a huge crowd of people, been welcomed by them, and welcomed them in return. It had felt like a kind of heaven, and showed me that some sort of togetherness was possible, if even for a short time.
Peter Gabriel was on that evening, but I had had enough.
I went back to my car and drove home.
I went to other festivals, but nothing quite compared to that Glastonbury.
The Stonehenge festival was a far darker affair.
As you arrived you were met by a cordon of police who let you through, but went no further, tacitly declaring the festival site to be off limits for them.
As a result drugs were sold openly on the site.
"Hot knives here 50p a go," coke and acid were freely available too.
The music was mainly heavy metal, and bikes revved up angrily all over the place.
I didn't stay the night.

The hippie festival scene is an odd plant that flourishes briefly and then withers away. You cannot keep hold of it, and when you try and relate it to others it seems like a drug induced self-satisfied fantasy.
Some people tried to keep it going all year round with various camps in Wales or around Totnes, but the magic of the tepee tends to be tempered by rain and the cold.
There was even a "convoy" of buses that travelled around from site to site full of what were to become known as "crusties". People who just let themselves go into dreadlocks, cut off jeans

and army boots. For all I know they are still out there.
But to those of us who have felt it, the memory of those hippy
times is still very sweet.

The important thing to do is to start

I began my own practice with the Lord's Prayer and have since developed it from there.

The key thing in developing a practice is to do what *you* feel comfortable with.

I started by saying those words through, and then sitting in silence for five minutes. It was amazing how still I felt for that short period of time. Gradually over the years I have added to this time – 5 minutes here and 5 minutes there. I now have a practice that lasts for an hour. I am lucky in that I can fit it into my day. (There is the old story of the businessman who was asked about his spiritual practice. "I do it once a day for 20 minutes, unless I am really busy – then I do it twice a day.")

I find that people are more comfortable talking about their sex lives than they are talking about their spiritual practice.

I practice once a day in the morning after breakfast. It has become so routine that I do not even consider whether or not I am going to do it.

I give myself two days off a week (usually Friday and Saturday). It is great to feel that you can have a break from the practice. I also drop my practice when I go on holiday.

I start by thinking over the previous day and quietly giving thanks for whatever has happened, good or bad. I also try to deal with any issues that I am facing at the time and that I am worried about.

I then use the *Collect for Purity*, an amazing set of words written by Thomas Cranmer in the 16th Century.

Like the Lord's Prayer it never fails to move me.

Almighty God,
unto whom all hearts be open,
all desires known,
and from whom no secrets are hid:
Cleanse the thoughts of our hearts
by the inspiration of your Holy Spirit,
that I may perfectly love you,
and worthily magnify your holy Name:
through Christ our Lord. Amen.

Almighty God,
The other that exists within us

unto whom all hearts be open,
Who knows all my thoughts

all desires known,
Everything I want

and from whom no secrets are hid:
Even those bits I do not like to admit to myself.

Cleanse the thoughts of our hearts
Make my heart pure

by the inspiration of your Holy Spirit,
Through contact with that part of yourself which is in me

that I may perfectly love you,
That I may fully give myself to you so that all my actions
conform to your will

and worthily magnify thy holy Name:
And your light will shine through me to others

through Christ our Lord.
Through your sacred influence

Amen.
So be it.

These words put my mind into exactly the right place.

I follow that with 30 minutes of meditation. Then 5 minutes of contemplation on the nature of the Christ. After that I will read something (usually from the Bible) and think about it. I will then think about those in my life that need help and follow that with the Lord's Prayer. I will then read another passage, and think about the day ahead. I finish by reading a poem.

The whole thing takes an hour, and I have a watch with a timer that "pings" to tell me when one section is finished and it is time to move on.

It has taken me 30 years to build that up, so don't think, "I could never do that, so there is no point in starting." I started with 10 minutes, you could start with 5. The important thing to do is to start. And when you find you have given up doing it, have the courage to start again, and again, and again.

When you have a practice, it gives you the confidence that you have at least given house room to that supreme being. You may not feel that you have made contact every time; however, if you do it in earnest, you will always get through, whether you know it or not. That's just the way it works.

The key thing is to be doing it. You then know that you are co-operating, and you are giving life the opportunity to guide you and show you what to do next.

Developing consciousness is something active. It requires perseverance day after day. It is the process of continually looking within in order to find out what to do on the outside. All of us have the opportunity for guidance in our lives; we just have to log on in order to download the updates, so to speak.

If nothing else it gives you confidence that you are "in the game". You are allowing yourself to be led, and therefore in whatever situation you find yourself, there is a way through.

As I said at the beginning of this book, you are never in the wrong place – you always have the opportunity to enable your life to lead you to what is ultimately wholesome and nourishing, or you can go your own way.

Meditation

We are all beginners at meditation. No matter how long you have been doing it, you are always starting from scratch.

If you look in any bookshop you will see yard of books dedicated to explaining the practice of one form of meditation or another.

Meditation is the practice we use to still the mind. It involves a point of focus – some use the breath or a special word – upon which the mind is trained, so as not to rush off into all the thoughts it normally entertains moment by moment. It is as simple as that. All the complications come from trying to work out what happens to you when you meditate.

I am not going to go into a huge amount of detail here about how to meditate – there are plenty of other books for that (see the booklist at the back of this book). Suffice to say that you should sit in a chair, or on a stool with a straight back and with your eyes closed (there are variations to this, but I am keeping it simple). You then begin to focus on your breath (I am going to use this as an example). Follow your breath in, and out, sensing it at the same time as it moves through your nostrils.

In and out. In and out. Just focus on your breath, not your thoughts.

You cannot stop yourself thinking. You can just stop yourself following those thoughts through. Instead of following them, just notice them. For example, if you find yourself thinking, "I must remember to buy some bread," don't follow that thought with, "OK I'll get some in the supermarket this afternoon, I'll take the car… " Otherwise five minutes later you will realise that you have stopped following your breath.

Instead, when you think, "I must remember to buy some bread," follow it with, "I notice I am thinking about bread," and go straight back to your breath.

Just stay with your breath. What that does is keep you in the present moment – still, not rushing away with a thought. It makes you mindful, and enables you to notice what is going on in that present moment. And it breaks the power that the mind has to make you do things unconsciously. The more you train your mind in meditation, the more conscious you will be of your mind in everyday life.

That is the basic practice of meditation. Scientists have observed that it lowers stress rates and creates healthier metabolism in the body.

What else it does is what the discussion is all about. Different techniques claim that they have different results. Buddhist "loving kindness meditation" purports to increase the amount of loving kindness in your life and in the lives of those around you. Christian Meditation puts you in touch with God – Psalm 46 says, "Be still and know that I am God."

If you are new to meditation, the first thing to do is to find a technique that suits you. Try loads, do workshops and see what works.

I began with 5 minutes of silence. I just observed my thoughts – I call it "sewage treatment" meditation. I would just sit and watch myself thinking, allowing my mind to churn out thought after thought without stopping it. It is a bit like a sewage treatment plant in that eventually my mind would calm down and I would have a few clear moments.

I did this method of meditation for about 10 years and it

served me well. I increased the time of my meditation from 5 minutes to about 20 minutes in those 10 years.

I then went on to using a 'word' – focusing on saying that word over and over again (a mantra). Rather than focussing on my breath, I focussed on saying the word. The word I used was Maranatha. It is Aramaic and it means "Come Christ".

Subsequently I have used other words, and at the time of writing I am using a focus on my breath. I now meditate, as a part of my practice, for 30 minutes.

For me it is about giving up my need to constantly make a comment about everything and anything that happens in my life. I simply bypass my mind by concentrating on my breath; noticing when I think of anything, but not following through on the thought. By doing this I manage to stay in the present moment and become still.

I do not always succeed and often go off into flights of fantasy, about one thing or another, eventually bringing myself back to my breath.

In meditation you are not trying to "get anywhere". You are not meditating in order to have any special experience. You are already having an experience, the experience of being in the present, practicing meditation. That is the only experience we are looking to have. As I said before, the reward for sitting in silence is sitting in silence.

The real benefits from meditation come as you are going about your day. You find yourself calmer, less prone to flying off the handle, and more able to watch your mind as it helps you negotiate your way through the day.

Meditation is an aid to developing consciousness. As an athlete trains in order to run the race, so you can use meditation in order to develop your consciousness.

Aged 33 – "Anyone but Thatcher"

When David Owen finished speaking there was no one to take him home.

I drove the smartest car we had in our group. It was a Rover 827, and it had the right feel for driving one of the leaders of the three political parties that were fighting it out in that year's General Election.

I brought the car round to the front of the venue – a 1000 seat sports hall in Southampton. Four of us had been on the bill for the rally, and David had spoken last. He was tired and had to get back to his home just outside Oxford; a four hour drive that would not see him in bed before 2.30am.

There is nothing more exhausting, politically, than a general election. You only have two months, so every hour of every day counts – you never stop.

Rallies, press conferences, putting up posters, canvassing, team building and, most important of all, deciding what to do next.

At every juncture there are always at least five things that could be done: the trick is to pick the right one to focus on.

For me the right one was driving David Owen home.

Access to a party leader, on his own, for three hours, when you are a merely a lowly campaign manager looking after an unwinnable constituency over 100 miles from London does not put you very high on the political pecking order; so you have to grab your chances when you get them.

David Owen is an incredibly nice guy.

He was dog-tired, and I am sure the last thing he wanted to do was make polite conversation with his driver as we drove deeper into the night; but that is exactly what he did, periodically winding down his window to keep himself awake.

After about half an hour of niceties he suddenly turned to me and said, "What do you think we should do about Thatcher?"

I was stunned. Here was a leader of one of the main British parliamentary parties asking me, at least 3,000 places down the pecking order from him, what he should do.

Was he really interested, or was this just more small talk to keep him awake? I wasn't really sure why he wanted to stay awake anyway. I would have gone to sleep and let the guy next to me do the driving ages ago.

What would I do about Thatcher?

I began to ramble incoherently until I found a direction that seemed to make sense and struck out along that path.

"The thing about Thatcher is her arrogance. No one likes it. We have to find a way of uniting everyone else behind that. Make it a sort of "Anyone but Thatcher" election. Appeal to that aspect of the electorate that likes consensus and unity."

It made sense to me at around 1.00 in the morning.

He liked it, and so I let myself build on the idea.

"What we should offer people is a Government of National Unity. Make it look as if the SDP/ Liberal Alliance (that was his party at the time) could occupy a loftier place in British Politics. Offer the electorate a chance of 'politics without the politics'."

He liked that too.

And so we both rambled on, reshaping that face of British politics in a Rover 827 travelling at about 80 miles per hour between Southampton and Oxford.

Eventually in the swirling mist, that only seems to come out in the deepest dark of the night, we drove through his gates and up to his rather large house.

David opened the car door and threw himself out in the way of someone who was either drunk or half asleep.

He grabbed his bag and stuck his head back inside. "Thanks very much for the lift and the chat," he shouted, and slammed the door. Without looking back he strode towards his front door and disappeared. I turned the car and headed for London.

When you get to bed at about four am you have permission to

sleep in, even during an election, so it was twelve when I came
out of the kitchen with a bowl of cereal to watch the midday
news.
The screen swirled from black into colour revealing an image of
David Owen with David Steel walking towards the camera.
"And at their morning press conference, the two Davids laid out
their strategy for the next phase of this election," pronounced the
voice-over.
The camera focused in on David Owen who looked straight at
the camera and said,
"What this country is looking for is a Government of National
Unity. We need to demonstrate that we can be above the normal
politics and offer something different..."
And so I had my first insight as to how policy was formed within
the British political system.

All eternity seems to have become ours in this one placid and breathless contact

"The simple enjoyment of the truth."[14]

That is how Thomas Aquinas, the 13th Century Dominican monk, described meditation. And yet there are many different interpretations of the purposes and benefits of the practice of meditation.

There is a certain amount of discussion as to the difference between meditation and contemplation, but for our purposes here we are treating them as one and the same. We are talking about the practice of witnessing "what is so" (i.e. the truth), without becoming involved with that which we are witnessing.

This is how James Finley describes it in his book *Christian Meditation*:[15]

"Meditative experience thinks nothing. It gazes deeply into the

nature of thought.

Meditative experience wills nothing. It gazes deeply into the nature of willing, and of all desire.

Meditative awareness believes nothing. It gazes deeply into the nature of belief.

Meditative awareness remembers nothing; it gazes deeply into the nature of memory.

Meditative experience feels nothing; it gazes deeply into the nature of feelings… Gazing deeply into the nature of ego consciousness meditative experience transcends ego consciousness.

You get the picture. Like the process of gazing at the pattern earlier in this book, meditative consciousness is a way of being conscious of the process of being conscious.

Some take it even further than that. If you are gazing at the very essence of consciousness, then, in effect, you are gazing at that divine consciousness.

Thomas Merton the 20th Century Trappist Monk says in his book *New Seeds of Contemplation*:[16]

"Contemplative prayer (meditation) *is a deep and simplified spiritual activity in which the mind and will rest in a unified and simplified concentration upon God, turned to Him, intent upon Him, and absorbed in His own light, with a simple gaze which is perfect adoration because it silently tells God that we have left everything else and desire even to leave our own selves for His sake, and that He alone is important to us, He alone is our desire and our life and nothing else can give us any joy."*

This view of meditation says that there is more going on in the process than simply stilling the mind. It says that by stilling the mind and gazing upon the manifestation of divine consciousness, you are actually coming into the presence of God. And that by doing so you are opening yourself to being transformed by the perfect purposes of God's will. You are perfectly conforming to those purposes, and by doing that you open yourself to being transformed by God, as a part of those purposes.

Which is not something you can think about during meditation. You just have to let those thoughts go too and simply be in that present moment. All the transformation, if it happens, will manifest gradually (or maybe suddenly) in our daily lives.

In speaking of the effects of meditation Thomas Merton goes further:[16]

"A door opens in the centre of our being and we seem to fall through it into immense depths which, although they are infinite, are accessible to us; all eternity seems to have become ours in this one placid and breathless contact."

And so we are back to witnessing that divine consciousness that is within us.

The paradox of meditation is that we often enter into it to experience this wonderful door opening, but it is not something that we could, or should, hope for in our practice; the benefit of doing the practice is doing the practice. And yet this door sometimes opens. When it does so it is a gift. It is not something that we can make happen, nor should we try to do so. It is a card that some of us are dealt in life, and if it appears in our hand, then we have to play it very carefully. It has the power to destroy as well as to nurture. It all depends on how we choose to use it.

Meditation is just a practice. One of many different practices that people use in developing consciousness. We have only really been able to scratch the surface here, and you will find much more on those bookshelves in the library. The key thing is to try it. If it does not suit you, than drop it, but over the years I have felt an increasing sense of peace and confidence through using it.

Rarely am I able to turn my mind off. I have one of those minds that just goes on and on. Meditation has helped me with that. It puts my mind out of control and allows something else to come through. Something that can heal and bring wholeness, something that brings me back to who I really am in that divine consciousness. It is the one place I know where I cannot be corrupt.

Out of our sleep and into the wakefulness of full consciousness

I started this book saying that dogs hear more, cats see more, so it stands to reason that there must be more.

I finish it by saying that there is more, but it is more of who you are, rather than more of something else.

The search to develop our consciousness takes us round in a circle so that we come to realise that it is our consciousness that is, in fact, developing us, rather than the other way round.

Our decision to engage in the process gives our consciousness the permission it needs to lead us out of our sleep and into the wakefulness of full consciousness. Consciousness of that part of ourselves that is shared by all; a divine consciousness which is itself a gift, and a part of that supreme being that some of us have come to call God.

Bede Griffiths says:[17]

"For most people the very idea of God has ceased to have any meaning. It is like the survival from a half-forgotten mythology. Before it can begin to have any meaning for them, they have to experience his reality in their lives. They will not be converted by words or arguments, for God is not merely an idea or a concept in philosophy; he is the very ground of existence. We have to encounter him as a fact of our existence before we can be persuaded to believe in him. To discover God is not to discover an idea, but to discover oneself. It is to awake to that part of our existence which has been

hidden from sight and which one refuses to recognise. The discovery
may be painful; it is like going through a kind of death. But it is the
one thing which makes life worth living."

Much of the talk of 'God' and 'supreme being' and 'divine
consciousness' are just words that we inadequately use to
describe the indescribable. I have used words that I am familiar
with, however, different traditions will use different words.

Once you get into arguing one form of words against another
you are into the subject of comparative religion, which is a
different book.

This book is about developing consciousness. Trying to find
our "what is" by looking inside at our experience, and looking
out at the experience of others. That sort of comparison enables
us to make a judgement about what is true for us.

What we then go on to say that we *believe* about that truth,
what we deduce from that truth, lies in the religious domain and
not here.

It is enough, for the purpose of this book, to look to ourselves.
Once we have done that, then we can reach out to others and
share what we have learnt, as I have tried to do in this book.

I finish this section with one more quote from Thomas Merton
which gives one picture of what this whole process entails:[16]

"God utters me like a word containing a partial thought of himself.
A word can never comprehend the voice that uttered it.
But if I am true to the concept that God utters in me, if I am true to
the thought of Him I was meant to embody, I shall be full of His
actuality and find him everywhere in myself, and find myself
nowhere.
I shall be lost in Him: that is I shall find myself. I shall be saved."

Present Day

Not to come last – that was the big hope.

All those words about doing your best and just enjoying it count for nothing as you look down those twin tracks of your lane and realise that the next 10 seconds marks the difference between humiliation and merely not being noticed.

On one side the school, merciless, waiting for the slightest weakness that could be used as a stick to beat one with for the rest of term. On the other the parents, armed with thousands of pounds of recording equipment to capture each millisecond of the trial ahead. Everyone expectant, waiting to see their children pitted against each other.

As the teacher raised the gun there was a hush like that before an execution.

Sweat and nervousness to the point of vomiting.

And I was not even running the race.

My 6 year old son was there in the line-up with his arm held out in front of him, like Superman about to go into flight, as if this would give him a better start.

I looked at him and all that was in front of him.

Not just the lane, but the life. The years of school that were to come; the victories and the humiliations he would have to undergo. The expectations and the disappointments that he was going to have.

And I felt for him. The ache of a parent who would be willing to undergo their child's pain to spare them all the suffering.

But without pain, there is no joy, just like there is no joy without pain. They are two sides of the same coin. Those we love dearest, we will at some time be parted from. And that parting will inevitably lead to another joy, as yet unidentified.

I saw all this for my son, as my mother no doubt saw for me.

She sat next to me now. All our memories held between us.

Next to her were my wife and my 4 year old daughter.

It is only when you look back that you can see what really formed you. Those moments that brought life into focus, establishing a precedent from which all subsequent experiences are judged.

Our lives become about those precedents, deciding what works for us, and then trying to live by what we have learnt.

That is the very nature of developing consciousness. Discovering the choices we have and then making decisions about those choices, rather than being swept along by the tide of what everyone else is doing.

The gun went off and the parents exploded into a roar of encouragement that momentarily startled the children.

"Come on, Angus," one of the fathers screamed, his red face signalling the effort he was expecting his son to put into winning. "You can do it. Push, push, push! That's it, keep going."

I too shouted for my son, video camera clamped to one eye and gesticulating encouragement with the other arm.

In the end he did not come last. Just somewhere near the back with a group of five others. Peace with honour!

I had been so excited that I turned the video camera off rather than on at the beginning and so missed recording any part of the race.

When I looked back at the film, there he was getting ready to go, and then suddenly there he was going over the line.

Like our lives when we look back at them.

There we are at the beginning, taking what seems ages to grow up and be able to do all the things we see grownups do, and then suddenly there we are again, almost the end.

And in the looking back, there is always so much that we could never have imagined.

The horizons that we aim for in life are often limited by our imagination.

If we let go and allow life to lead us, not trying to get what we want, but wanting what we get, then often life will take us somewhere quite unexpected.

Thirty years ago my imagined best future would have included a Bentley Continental, some fabulous home and endless diversions to keep me happy.

And here I am as an Anglican priest, married with children.

Not much money, but wealthier than my wildest dreams and with a sense of contentment that I am almost embarrassed by.

How did I get here? I sometimes wonder.

But that is another story.

More Information

For more information about The Developing Consciousness Course or Nicholas Vesey, and for an opportunity to share your own spiritual experiences go to

www.developingconsciousness.net

My Thanks

I would like to thank everyone who has helped me with this book.

Especially to my wife Heather without whom... well goodness knows where I would be now. For reading, reflecting, correcting and allowing me to bare my soul, and therefore a little bit of hers too.

To Richard Rohr and those from the Center for Action and Contemplation in Albuquerque, New Mexico, who gave us somewhere to stay and looked after us while I wrote.

To all my friends who kindly read the book and gave me such useful feedback.

To those from school, university, advertising, Exegesis, the church and other parts of my life who have given me much of the inspiration that has led to this book.

To Tim Lenton and all at St Augustine's for their support of the project.

To Omer-li Cohen for wonderful help and advice.

And to you for taking the time to read it and therefore making it all worthwhile!

Booklist

The Power of Now by Eckhart Tollë
Great book, covers the same sort of material as this book, but from a slightly different perspective.

Awareness by Anthony de Mello
Great for looking at the nature of our awareness, interesting exercises to help you

The Golden String by Bede Griffiths
Autobiography of this Christian Monk who founded an ashram in India

A New Vision of Reality by Bede Griffiths
How he sees life.

The Prophet by Khalil Gibran
Short pearls of wisdom

Everything Belongs *by Richard Rohr*
Living the mystical life

The Perennial Philosophy by Aldous Huxley
Seminal work on the nature of religion

New Seeds of Contemplation by Thomas Merton
Christian Mystical Classic

The Tao Te Ching Stephen Mitchell (trans)
Classic Chinese text

And finally three fabulous books on Christian Meditation from three different perspectives

Christian Meditation by James Finley

Into the Silent Land by Martin Laird

Centering Prayer and Inner Awakening by Cynthia Bourgeault

Notes

1. Sutherland, NS, ed. *The International Dictionary of Psychology,* NY: Continuum, 1989

2. Philip K Dick, *"How to Build a Universe That Doesn't Fall Apart Two Days Later",* 1978

3. Sogyal Rinpoche, *The Tibetan Book of Living and Dying,* Rider, 1992, p. 31

4. His Holiness the Dalai Lama, *The Good Heart,* Rider, 2002, p. 102

5. Albert Einstein quoted www.nlpu.com/Articles/Sept_11.html

6. Rowan Williams, *Silence and Honeycakes,* Lion Books, 2004, p. 22

7. Aldous Huxley, *The Perennial Philosophy,* Triad Grafton, 1989, p. 9

8. Bede Griffiths, *Return to the Centre,* Fount, 1978, p. 74

9. Stephen Mitchell trans. *Tao Te Ching,* Harper and Row NY, 1988

10. Rowan Williams, *Ponder These Things,* Canterbury Press, 2002, p. 46

11. Eckhart Tollë, *The Power of Now,* Hodder and Stoughton, 1999, p. 79

12. Holy Bible, New International Version

13. Khalil Gibran, *The Prophet,* Pan Books, 1991, p. 70

14. Thomas Aquinas quoted by John Main and noted by Brian V Johnstone CSSR from the 63.2.2004 issue of Review for Religious

15. James Finley, *Christian Meditation,* HarperSanFrancisco, 2005, p. 63

16. Thomas Merton, *New Seeds of Contemplation,* Shambhala, 2003, pp. 247, 230 & 39

17. Bede Griffiths, *The Golden String,* Medio Media, 2003, p. 4

Illustrations

Cover calligraphy by Rachel Lankester.
The Chinese character on the front of the book is the character for the word 'light'.

Cover art by Chen Hong.

CHANGE
MAKERS
BOOKS

Changemakers Books

TRANSFORMATION

Transform your life, transform your world - Changemakers Books publishes for individuals committed to transforming their lives and transforming the world. Our readers seek to become positive, powerful agents of change. Changemakers Books inform, inspire, and provide practical wisdom and skills to empower us to write the next chapter of humanity's future. If you have enjoyed this book, why not tell other readers by posting a review on your preferred book site. Recent bestsellers from Changemakers Books are:

Integration
The Power of Being Co-Active in Work and Life
Ann Betz, Karen Kimsey-House
Integration examines how we came to be polarized in our dealing with self and other, and what we can do to move from an either/or state to a more effective and fulfilling way of being.
Paperback: 978-1-78279-865-1 ebook: 978-1-78279-866-8

Lead Yourself First!
Indispensable Lessons in Business and in Life
Michelle Ray
Are you ready to become the leader of your own life? Apply simple, powerful strategies to take charge of yourself, your career, your destiny.
Paperback: 978-1-78279-703-6 ebook: 978-1-78279-702-9

Burnout to Brilliance
Strategies for Sustainable Success
Jayne Morris
Routinely running on reserves? This book helps you transform
your life from burnout to brilliance with strategies for
sustainable success.
Paperback: 978-1-78279-439-4 ebook: 978-1-78279-438-7

The Master Communicator's Handbook
Teresa Erickson, Tim Ward
Discover how to have the most communicative impact in this
guide by professional communicators with over 30 years of
experience advising leaders of global organizations.
Paperback: 978-1-78535-153-2 ebook: 978-1-78535-154-9

Future Consciousness
A Path to Purposeful Evolution
Tom Lombardo
How do our unique conscious minds reflect and amplify
nature's vast evolutionary process? This book reveals how we
can flourish in the flow of evolution and create a prosperous
future for ourselves, human society and the planet.
Paperback: 978-1-78099-985-2 ebook: 978-1-78279-070-9

Modern Machiavelli
Troy Bruner and Philip Eager
Modern Machiavelli will teach you smart, social tactics to
advance your career and improve your relationships. This book
explains how to successfully manage conflict, influence others,
and understand the overt and covert dynamics of interpersonal
power.
Paperback: 978-1-78535-611-7 ebook: 978-1-78535-612-4

Soccer Thinking for Management Success
Peter Loge
Success used to look like football. Now success looks like soccer.
Soccer is 90 minutes of systems thinking in action. This book is
by a soccer fan and player who has spent a career building and
running teams and organizations. He draws on insights from
leaders, known and not-so-well-known, who use soccer thinking
to succeed.
Paperback: 978-1-78535-754-1 ebook: 978-1-78535-755-8

Readers of ebooks can buy or view any of these bestsellers by
clicking on the live link in the title. Most titles are published in
paperback and as an ebook. Paperbacks are available in
traditional bookshops. Both print and ebook formats are
available online.

Find more titles and sign up to our readers' newsletter at
http://www.johnhuntpublishing.com/transformation
Follow us on Facebook at
https://www.facebook.com/Changemakersbooks